COME WIND, COME WEATHER

The Present Experience of the Church in China

By

LESLIE T. LYALL

The title of this book is taken from John Bunyan's
pilgrim hymn, "He Who Would Valiant Be."

> He who would valiant be
> 'Gainst all disaster,
> Let him in constancy
> Follow the Master.
> There's no discouragement
> Shall make him once relent
> His first avowed intent
> To be a pilgrim.
>
> Who would true valor see,
> Let him come hither;
> One here will constant be,
> *Come wind, come weather.*

MOODY PRESS
CHICAGO

Printed in the United States of America

CONTENTS

PREFACE

THIS BOOK is not concerned with politics, with economics, with sociology, or with ideology—except indirectly. It has one aim—to set out in an unbiased documentary manner the way in which the Communist government has handled the Protestant church in China.

The more we study the documents and statements of the official church leaders, the clearer we see that the direction in which the Protestant church has been moving since 1950 has been dictated by the People's Government. It has not been determined, as some still think, by the spontaneous, freely chosen policies of the Christian church itself. On the contrary, a carefully planned and cleverly executed government scheme to immobilize the church without destroying it entirely and to render it ineffective while apparently leaving it "free" has been imposed. The state legislature and the state police have worked closely with the officially recognized Protestant organization: those whom the organization has denounced or condemned have been arrested by the state police, tried by "People's Courts" and punished in various ways by the state authorities.

A comparison with the circumstances of the arrest, trial, and crucifixion of our Lord Jesus Christ is inevitable. What were, in the case of Jesus Christ, purely religious issues, were made to appear political issues in order to secure His condemnation and death. Many Chinese Christians, too, who have been concerned only to remain loyal to Jesus Christ, have been made to appear as political traitors and criminals in the eyes of the world in order to bring them to judgment and punishment.

If at first sight the following record appears to have political overtones, it is because the Communist government has deliberately adopted the policy of using the Christian church as a political tool and for political propaganda, while at the same time rendering her spiritually impotent. It is quite impossible to tell the story in any detail without becoming involved to some extent in political affairs. No one, whoever he may be, can live in the New China without becoming deeply involved in politics. There are no such things as neutrality or disinterestedness.

Many people throughout the world are still seeing the church situation in China through a propaganda smoke screen which the Chinese authorities have ingeniously put up. Anyone who travels among the churches in the homeland soon becomes aware of this. There is a general idea that things are not so bad for Christians as was expected.

It is therefore in the interest of truth and of the greatest concern to missions and churches in other Asian and African countries living beneath the long shadows of Communism that the facts should be made crystal clear. For China may well be a blueprint of the methods which Communist authorities will adopt elsewhere.

But—most important of all—only a clear understanding of the real situation as distinct from the half-truths and deliberate deceptions of Communist well-wishers and fellow-travelers will drive the church of Jesus Christ to her knees on behalf of its members in China. There is abundant evidence of a growing prayer concern for the Chinese church, and recent leaflets throwing light on the situation have had a remarkable circulation.

This book attempts to fill out the picture, in the hope that it will call forth an even greater volume of believing prayer for Christians in China.

Chapter 1

UNEASY PEACE

CHINA TODAY is a land of exciting progress. The population has been mobilized on a mammoth scale. Enormous dams are aiding the greatly needed river conservation. New factories are producing everything from airplanes and automobiles to a growing variety of consumer goods. A magnificent road-and-rail bridge at Hankow is the first ever to span the mighty Yangtze. There is a rapidly increasing railway mileage, a vast building program, and an impressive literacy progress. Pest elimination and scientific farming have contributed to a mounting agricultural production. The cleaning up of vice, the improvement in health services and a hundred things beside, clamor to the world that China under Communism is a "workers' paradise."

At last, it is suggested, the Chinese people have a system consonant with the dignity of man. The English-language illustrated magazines, magnificently produced in Peking, present a picture of a people relaxed, happy, and free under beneficent rulers who are depicted to be the object of universal admiration and even affection.

But is this the whole truth, or is there another side? For the Christian at least—yes, there is most decidedly another side to the picture. The Christian is never primarily concerned with purely material values, though he is not indifferent to them—his outlook is determined by spiritual factors. And so, life in a materialist's paradise confronts him with a host of complex problems.

7

For twenty-seven years the Chinese Communist Party had been on its way to power. After its organization in 1921, it grew within the Nationalist Party. Then, in 1927, following the Northern March from Canton to the Yangtze of the armies under General Chiang Kai-shek, the Nationalists broke with the Communists, who set up a separate capital in Hankow. A long and bitter civil war ensued, the main fighting taking place in the province of Kiangsi, where the first Chinese soviets were set up and where the Christian churches suffered severely.

Finally, as the Nationalists gained the upper hand, the Communist armies escaped from encirclement and undertook the epic Long March through the western border regions northward to the province of Shensi. Out of an army of 100,000 that set out, a mere 30,000 survived the rigors and privations of the journey; among them were the present rulers of China. In Yenan, in northern Shensi, these men set up a "provisional government" and planned their next moves. War with Japan was the outcome.

When war broke out in 1937, the Communists accepted an alliance with the Nationalists against the common enemy. Both armies faced the Japanese with great courage. But the Nationalists were committed to orthodox warfare. They won notable victories and suffered tragic defeats at the hands of an enemy superior in training and equipment. The Communists, on the other hand, including the famous Eighth Route Army, engaged in guerrilla warfare behind the Japanese lines, and in areas supposedly occupied by the Japanese armies. These were times when missionaries found their sympathies with all who fought the common enemy, including the courageous young men and women of the guerrilla forces, in their fight against a ruthless foe. They were often able to render medical aid and advice to grateful Communist detachments.

But as the war progressed, the Communists kept in mind

the advice of their teacher Lenin, given in an earlier war: "The transformation of the war into a civil war is the one good watchword of the proletariat." And so, when the long war against Japan came to its tragic but victorious end, the old civil war flared up.

Meanwhile, naval transport vessels were chartered to carry back to China whole boatloads of missionaries who had been snatching a furlough after internment or war strain. Hundreds of missionaries poured back into China to resume their varied Christian activities, from Mongolia in the north to the tribal area of the southwest, and from the Tibetan frontier to the Yellow Sea. Those were days of great expectations and abounding optimism. The wartime work in the west among refugee students had borne fruit. For the first time in the history of the Chinese church, university students everywhere were not only showing a remarkable interest in the Gospel and being soundly converted, but they were offering themselves in large numbers for the Christian ministry and as missionaries to their own people. Bible colleges and theological seminaries had never been so full. One significant feature was the coming into existence of a number of missionary societies founded by Chinese, financially supported by Chinese Christians and consisting entirely of Chinese personnel. Many young men and women left the comfort of the big cities near the coast to take the Gospel to the Mongolian and Tibetan border regions, to Central Asia and to the tribes of the southwest. Churches throughout the country were throbbing with life. There was in many places an atmosphere akin to revival. The church seemed to be on the verge of a period of consolidation and unlimited growth.

The future looked bright.

Chapter 2

EASY VICTORY

STUDENT WORK IN PEKING, with its numerous universities and colleges, was enjoying unprecedented blessing. In 1947 the Christian students were holding their second summer conference beneath the walls of the Imperial Summer Palace—wonderful days of salvation and revival and the most joyful Christian fellowship! The Western Hills were just a mile or two away. Not far beyond were the outposts of the encroaching Red Army. Peking had become almost an island on the shores of which the threatening waves were already breaking. The red leaves of autumn came to the trees of the Western Hills and as usual attracted many lovers of beauty. The President of China himself decided to visit that lovely place. Autumn melancholy was in the air. And he must have known that he was visiting that beauty spot for the last time. For him it was farewell to Peking!

That winter of 1947-8 found the lovely old temples of the ancient capital built by Genghis Khan in the 13th century crowded with student refugees from Communist-occupied areas. These and thousands of Peking students were sharply divided into pro-Communists and anti-Communists. Underground activities of every kind went on. Even Christian students experimented with Communist-style "self-criticism meetings"! There were banned demonstrations and tragic shootings. Daily the pro-Communists became bolder. The Peking Youth for Christ Committee arranged what was possibly the largest evangelistic

10

campaign ever to have been held in Peking—an open-air mat stadium was erected on the former polo ground of the foreign embassies and the Gospel was faithfully preached to large numbers of people. This was in the nick of time.

Events began to move more quickly. Manchuria fell. The authority of the Central Government crumbled. The morale of the government troops was low. The fall of Peking became imminent. The garrison went through the motions of preparation to defend the city. The polo ground which had seen the crowds attentive to the Gospel now became an emergency airfield. All to no purpose! One fine day, Communist troops quietly marched into the city that was soon to become the capital of the "New China."

En route to join my family in South China, after leaving Peking with a Chinese companion, I had to force my way on to a train for which all too many refugees had waited for hours. The only way in was through the nearest window! All the seats were occupied and every square inch in the aisles was crowded with bundles and bedding and the families of army officers. Those who failed to get *into* the train traveled on the roof or suspended themselves in hammocks beneath the coaches. The whole tragic business was symbolical of a demoralized nation. Wounded soldiers boldly taunted men in officers' uniforms: "Why aren't you at the front instead of running away with your wives and children?" There were high words, bitter recriminations, and sometimes blows.

South of the Yangtze River there were refugees everywhere. Schoolboys and schoolgirls from the north crowded every available temple. Many hearts were soft and open to the Gospel, for none knew if they would ever again see their homes or families.

The Communist armies were steadily moving south, carrying everything before them. Somehow there was a pathetic delusion abroad that they could never succeed in crossing the mighty Yangtze—broad and unbridged as it then was. Like a mesmerized rabbit helpless before a stoat, people openly said, "It can't happen here!" At a conference in the coastal city of Wenchow for leaders from the hundreds of country churches and the two large city churches, the subject was the First Epistle of Peter—an epistle written to steel believers for persecution and suffering. Yet to most it seemed unreal to think of the Communists ever reaching so far south.

The 1948 summer student conference was in progress in the grounds of one of the Shanghai universities when the news came that the Red armies had crossed the Yangtze and had captured Nanking. By that time the populace had become inured to disasters. The young people accepted the news with complete calm. They could only wait with resignation for whatever the future would bring. It could scarcely be worse than the past!

When Shanghai fell after several days of fierce fighting, the staff of the China Bible Seminary, adjoining the railroad station at Kiangwan, anxiously followed the course of the battle. They could not forget that this had already been a battlefield in the war against Japan and the seminary buildings had been destroyed by shellfire. At night they watched the distant artillery duel and listened to the rumble and roar of battle. A Chinese colonel and his troops had requisitioned the men's hostel and dug trenches in the grounds. Shanghai fell first. It was a day or two later before our turn came. One night the colonel sent for me. "The Communists will soon be here," he said. "We are about to withdraw and go to Taiwan, but do not trust the Communists! They will not interfere with you at first and will be very polite. On no account fall into the trap and be deceived by fair words. When they have gathered all the information they need, then after a year or perhaps two they will act. You are forewarned!"

Soon after the colonel and his troops had pulled out, a deafening roar shook every building within a radius of a mile, and for us the night became as day when the gasoline tanks in the athletic stadium a quarter of a mile away went up in flames with an enormous explosion. Sleep that night was fitful. There were small children and a hundred students to be considered. At dawn there was a sudden eruption of rifle and automatic gunfire all around us. Peering through the windows we watched Communist soldiers converging on the railroad station without opposition. We too had been "liberated"!

The Nationalist government leaders had already escaped to Taiwan, taking with them all the money in the Bank of China. In Taiwan they set up a refugee government. Their underpaid, demoralized armies had proved no match for the well-paid, well-fed, and well-disciplined Communist troops. Hankow, Chungking, Canton—all fell in rapid succession and the whole of China was virtually in Communist hands—"liberated"! It remained only to consolidate the victory. It had taken just twenty-eight years for the Communist Party to seize power through armed revolution. It had been a textbook victory.

Advance Communist propagandists had everywhere reassured the people that Communists would not interfere with religion. People in general accepted this assurance and events at first seemed to justify that confidence.

In the more remote and smaller places there was trouble over the commandeering of church premises for the use of the army. But on the whole, church life continued without much change. Missionaries were pleasantly surprised to find that they could stay on. Some became optimistic about the possibility of continuing missionary work in the New China. But I remembered the colonel's warning: ". . . they will not interfere with you at first and will be very polite, but on no account fall into the trap and be deceived by fair words!"

Quite evidently the Communist authorities needed time to consolidate their victory and to compile their records in preparation for the next stage. Chinese Christian leaders had few illusions. Some left the country while it was possible to do so. But the majority recognized that their destiny was linked with their own country and with the Christian church over which God had made them the shepherds. They therefore put personal safety aside. The measure of their courage and self-denial is seen in what some of them have since had to suffer.

Christian missionaries can be forgiven for thinking that they had perhaps misjudged the Communists. Evidences that the new government of China was efficient and honest were plentiful. Inflation was halted. Communications were restored. Economic life began to pick up. There was a new spirit of efficiency and enthusiasm in place of the apathy and disillusionment that had been prevalent. Even Shanghai, a city of three million people, seemed to present no problem in administration to these hitherto inexperienced administrators.

Then the battle for Korea began. The exciting rhythm of hip drums disturbed the quiet of the evenings. "Volunteers" were sent off to the front with great honor. And who could resist the attraction of the mammoth parades and the *yang-ko* dances—colorful, well-organized, exciting —whenever any excuse for a celebration came around?

The heart of a nation was throbbing once more!

Chapter 3

MANIFESTO OF BETRAYAL

O N June 30, 1950, a representative group of Christian leaders and missionaries were summoned to the Y.M.C.A. building in Shanghai to hear a report of a historic meeting in Peking between four church leaders[1] and high government officials. The conference had lasted for parts of three days and one night in May. This in itself was unprecedented—no government had ever paid the Christian church in China such a compliment. The four men had come away from the conference in high spirits, feeling flattered and optimistic. They now reported the three long discussions they had held with Mr. Chou En-lai, the Premier, and his colleagues.

The government leaders had explained that any troubles Christians may have experienced were due to the fact that in the eyes of the people the church was associated with foreign imperialism. It was therefore up to the church itself, the report continued, to purge itself of all imperialist taint and then it might hope to take its place honorably in the new Chinese society.

As everyone knew, the new Constitution contained a clause guaranteeing freedom of religious belief to all Chinese citizens, and the government was sincere in its intention to implement this guarantee. There was no

---

[1]Mr. Y. T. Wu, Manager and Editor of the Association Press (Y.M.C.A.); Mr. Liu Liang-mo, Secretary of the National Y.M.C.A.; the Rev. Tsui Hsien-hsiang, General Secretary of the Church of Christ in China; and the Rev. George Wu, General Secretary of the National Christian Council.

basic antagonism on the part of the government to the church itself, but only to the way in which it had been used as a tool for imperialistic designs in China. So the church leaders had been told, and so they reported to us. A significant phrase quoted from Premier Chou—"While China is putting its house in order it is undesirable for guests to be present"—was not lost on the missionaries!

Mr. Y. T. Wu then presented what he called the Church Manifesto. The broad terms of this document had been drawn up during the conference in May by the Premier and the delegation. The document pledged the Christian church to rid itself of all traces of imperialism, to give its first loyalty to the People's Government, and to maintain unquestioning obedience to the Communist Party. A committee was appointed to dot the "i's" and cross the "t's" in the actual wording, but no major criticism of the document as a whole was voiced. Late that evening the gist of the evening's proceedings was reported to the China Inland Mission Field Director, Mr. J. R. Sinton. His immediate reaction was, "This is the beginning of the end!" It was in fact the writing on the wall. *Heavenly Wind* published the accepted text in its issue of August 10 with the comment, "This Manifesto will have historic significance for Christianity in China."

Throughout Shanghai there began a drive to obtain the signatures of all Christians for the document. It was hoped eventually to obtain the signature of every Christian in China. On September 23 the full text of the Manifesto was published simultaneously in the daily papers all over China. As if by prearrangement, the local Communist cadres called on the local church leaders to inquire their reaction.

"You agree, of course?"

"Yes!"

"Then why do you still welcome the presence and help of these foreign imperialist missionaries?"

No government edict expelling missionaries! No direct action to interfere with their work! Just the subtle pressure on the Christians to act themselves. Sadly and fearfully they sent delegations to see the missionaries.

"We deeply appreciate all you have done for us in the past. But times have changed. In the New China it will be very difficult for us to work together"—an embarrased pause—"so perhaps it would be better if you gave up your Bible class. It might even be best if you didn't come to church at all!"

The missionaries bowed to the inevitable. It was "the will of the people"! Not that it was the same everywhere, but similar events were reported from all over China. The missionary societies correctly interpreted the growing mass of evidence. One by one they gave instructions to their missionaries to withdraw from China. Some left in 1950, but throughout 1951 the withdrawal was in full swing. All was going according to the government plan—and without a single government order!

But the withdrawal was made as difficult and as humiliating as possible. Before exit visas were granted, a public notice had to appear in the local press inviting anyone with claims against the missionaries to file them at once. A demand was made for the property deeds. Only when these formalities had been complied with were the missionaries free to leave. Some local person also had to stand as sponsor for each departing missionary and to guarantee their future good behavior! The People's Government in this way acquired a very large amount of valuable property—hospitals, universities, schools, and private residences. The churches were permitted to use what appeared adequate for their use. But henceforth education, medicine, orphanages, and charitable institutions of all kinds were to become the prerogative of the People's Government and they were removed from the sphere of Christian responsibility. Insofar as Christians engaged in any educational, medical, or philanthropic activities, it would henceforth be as ordinary citizens in the service of their country. As Christians their sole freedom was to believe in and to worship God.

A few missionaries endured prolonged trials before they eventually emerged (cf. *Green Leaf in Drought-Time,*[2] by Isobel Kuhn). Some suffered greatly. Some even lost their lives.

The Manifesto marked the end of over one hundred years of Protestant missionary work in China. Its proclamation was probably inevitable in the anxious atmosphere of 1950-51. To bow to the inevitable must have seemed the only way to insure the continued existence of the church itself. It was the price the government demanded for the "liberty" it promised, and it was a hard bargain. It is sad to reflect that no Christian leaders in China offered any protest against the elimination of their brethren in Christ from overseas, and that such a breach in Christian fellowship on purely national grounds should have been precipitated where no spiritual grounds existed.

It is sad, too, to think that they accepted what they very well knew to be totally untrue, the Communist "line" that foreign missionaries were nothing but tools of foreign imperialism. The missionary movement had made many mistakes. It certainly had been slow and hesitant to transfer full responsibility to the Chinese church. Individual missionaries were undoubtedly often overbearing and betrayed attitudes which were offensive to Chinese national pride. But these were not of deliberate or malicious intent. The motives of Christian missionaries were from the

---

[2]Moody Press, 1957, cloth and paper.

first pure—the love of Christ was the constraining motive behind all their activities. For the most part they enjoyed the affection and the confidence of the humble poor. They were friends to all and offered their services in the realm of education and medicine without ulterior motives. Contrary to popular belief, missionaries received neither recognition nor financial support from their governments. And yet intelligent Christian leaders were persuaded to accept a Manifesto which condemned the very movement to which the Chinese church owed its existence.

Ever since the publication of the Manifesto in 1950, "missionary imperialism" has been the dominant theme of all Communist propaganda. Throughout 1959 a committee of church leaders in Peking was collecting information from every congregation in China about "the use of the church by imperialism." This information had to be studied by all local Three-Self committees and then forwarded to Peking. There a comprehensive treatise was to be prepared on the basis of the information collected to celebrate ten years of Communist rule in China and ten years of freedom from "missionary imperialism."

Some may ascribe to Mr. Wu and his colleagues the best of motives in those early days of the Revolution. But he and his colleagues did not foresee that the noose prepared for the foreign missionary movement would one day become a Haman's gallows for the church!

Chapter 4

THE THREE-SELF PATRIOTIC
MOVEMENT

D URING THE LAND REFORM PERIOD in 1950, many country churches had been closed by government order
and had remained closed. But in 1951 and 1952 the various levels of government began ordering the churches to
reopen and the congregations to reassemble. Christians
lifted their heads again.

In April 1951, 158 church leaders were brought to Peking at government expense and met under the presidency
of a government official[1] to deal with "the disposal of the
properties of American-subsidized missionary groups in
China." A government spokesman, in his inaugural address, said: "The mission of the conference is to cut off
thoroughly all relations between the Christian church and
American imperialism and to help the patriotic Christians
to promote a new movement for independence, self-support, and independent propagation of the Faith, *so as to
realize the decision of the Government Administrative
Council.*" The Christian leaders were therefore left in no
doubt at all what the demands of the government on the
church were.

One outcome of this first national conference was the
creation of the "Oppose-America, Aid-Korea, Three-Self
Reform-Movement of the Church of Christ in China,"
often abbreviated to the "Three-Self Reform Church." A

---

[1]The Chairman of the Cultural, Education and Religious Bureaus of
the Government Administrative Council.

preparatory committee of twenty-five persons was elected to shape the future destiny of the church in China on the basis of the Manifesto. The new slogan adopted was "Love country: love church!" and in that order. Moreover, the church was to be self-governing, self-supporting, and self-propagating—the "Three Selfs." This formula was borrowed from the missionary movement of thirty years before, but was now given a new interpretation: self-governing meant freedom from imperialist control; self-supporting meant freedom from imperialist finance; and self-propagating meant preaching "the truth," not imperialist "poison." Unfortunately the missionary goal of independence of thirty years earlier had not been universally realized before the Communists came to power, and it was left to a Communist government to demand that the church should immediately achieve this status. All funds from America and Great Britain were to be refused henceforth. This naturally hit very hard the churches which had been dependent on such funds, especially those possessing large properties and institutions. There were, however, many churches which had previously achieved full autonomy, and for them the problem of self-support was already solved.

That first inaugural conference was significant for the way in which, in effect, the Chinese church was wedded to the secular state and became, through its official leaders, an important instrument in the hands of the state for the promotion of social developments and the industrialization of China. The socialist utopia which would result would in effect be the promised heaven on earth. Nothing was said about the essential spiritual needs of men: the witness of the church to spiritual realities and to the Person of Jesus Christ was evidently to be relegated to a very minor place in the church's program.

In the January 17, 1953 issue of *Heavenly Wind*, the

preparatory committee of the Three-Self Reform Church contributed the following summary of the achievements of the Movement as reported at the second anniversary celebrations in the late autumn of 1952:

1. The Christians and the churches of the whole nation have come to recognize America's imperialistic use of the church in its aggression in China. They are determined to cut off all relationships with America. They plan gradually to purify the church of imperialistic influences. They recognize the urgency and necessity of the Three-Self Reform.

2. The loyalty of Christians and their zeal for their nation has been raised very high. They recognize that love for one's country and love for the church are one and the same thing. Therefore all Christians fervently enter into all the efforts of the Oppose-America Aid-Korea Movement.

3. In the work of the Three-Self Reform Movement, the church has made progress and received valuable experience. Since the purging out of imperialistic influences and the establishment of the Three-Self Reform Church, the relationship between the church leaders and the Christians has become more congenial and united.

4. The spirit of unity under the banner of Oppose-America, Love-Your-Country, and the Three-Self Reform has been greatly increased and is highly honored and respected by the people. Because of this, many of the churches have fulfilled the requirements of becoming full-fledged members of the Three-Self Reform Church.

From this statement, discerning Christian readers in the most remote parts of China could see the trend of things. Others might have been deceived by the high-sounding phraseology, the careless use of the word "unity," and the flattering assurance of the growing status of the church in the nation.

The anxious and disturbing months of 1953 went by. The "Jesus Family," a significant Christian communal experiment, was dissolved. Then came the important conference of church delegates in Peking in 1954. They met from July 22 to August 6. The main event was Mr. Y. T. Wu's review of the accomplishments of four years. The delegates listened without enthusiasm to the by now familiar jargon:

> The principal accomplishments of the Three-Self Reform Movement during the past four years have been the freeing of the personnel, management and finances of the church from imperialistic control, the cutting off of imperialistic relations, the beginning of wiping out of imperialistic influence and the first steps in self-government, self-support, and self-propagation.[2]

The whole speech betrayed a mind obsessed with the delusion that from beginning to end the entire missionary movement in China had been one of imperialist aggression and that Chinese Christianity had consistently been its tool. There was venom in every line. Gutzlaff, Timothy Richard, Hudson Taylor, and others were singled out by name:

> These missionaries . . . misinterpreted the Scriptures, perverted Christian doctrine, nurtured unspeakable renegades within the church, created disunion and division within the church, and made Chinese Christians unconsciously breathe in the poison of imperialist thought.[3]

Words like these must surely have shocked some of those present! Mr. Wu ended by announcing that as the permanent church organization was now well established, the original title would "for the sake of unity" be dropped: a new title would take its place—"The Chinese Christian

[2]*Heavenly Wind*, August, 1954.
[3]Ibid.

Three-Self Patriotic Movement." It would seem that there had been widespread objection to the idea of "reform," a word which suggested interference in the internal affairs of the churches and even a modification of the creeds. Church spokesmen denied such aims and the necessary concession was made. The offending word was removed. No one could any longer object to a merely patriotic movement! But the sponsors of the Movement never for a moment abandoned their mission to reform the church: it was merely postponed for another four years. Meanwhile, the Movement undertook the task of summoning Christians to promote the socialization of society, to oppose the aggression of imperialism, to continue patriotic studies with a view to purging out completely all imperialistic influences and the poison of imperialist doctrine, and to preach a pure Gospel!

The first President of the Three-Self Movement was Mr. Y. T. Wu himself. During the late war with Japan he became anti-Nationalist and pro-Communist, even taking part in several movements which aimed at the overthrow of the Nationalist Government. His enthusiasm for the Communists grew after the war and he became an ardent student of Communist theory. His known sympathy for the Communists and his key position in the Y.M.C.A. made Mr. Wu an obvious government choice to head up the Three-Self Movement. This organization was designed to operate in relation to the Protestant churches as the agent of the Religious Affairs Bureau, a government department created to carry out the religious policies of the government. Writing in *Heavenly Wind* for June 30, 1958 under the title, "My Recognition of the Communist Party," Mr. Wu said:

> *Without the Communist Party there would not have been the Three-Self Movement of the Christian church,* nor the new life of the church, and we Christians would

not have received education in socialism and the opportunity to change our political standpoint and become one with the people as we march happily on the road to Socialism. . . . I love the Communist Party. . . . For over a hundred years imperialism had been using the Christian church to advance its aggressive designs. . . . And even today in the minds of not a few Christians there still remain the destructive poisons of imperialism and anti-Party, anti-Socialism thinking. As a tool of imperialism the church had become a force in the service of reactionary rulers. The church greatly needed cleansing, for without that cleansing there would be no future for her in New China. And so for several years now the Three-Self Movement has carried on this work of cleansing the church, but *this was a work which could not have been carried on without the support and direction of the Party*.

In plain words Mr. Wu states that the Three-Self Movement is not now and never has been a free or spontaneous expression of the church's life. He declares it to be the creation of the Communist Party, to be directed at the highest level by the Communist Party, and to be carrying out the intentions of the Communist Party. Mr. Wu had evidently become more keenly aware of that fact in 1959 than he was in 1951 at the birth of the Movement, for he concluded his article, written at the time when denominational distinctions were being broken up and the number of churches drastically reduced, by saying:

In the Great Leap Forward, I realize that I have fallen behind, I have not kept up with the times, and consequently feel that other people are moving too fast. I must thoroughly reform myself and stretch every nerve to press forward. I must come closer to the Party, have more confidence in it, and with the people of the whole country work to create the miracle of socialist reconstruction.

This then is the leader of the Movement. In 1953 he was honored and rewarded for his services by election to the Standing Committee of the People's Political Consultative Council, the Chinese legislative assembly. In the year or two following the publication of the Manifesto, Mr. Y. T. Wu, with his considerable prestige, and his colleagues made long and frequent journeys all over China in an all-out endeavor to win the support of all sections of the church. To many, Mr. Wu's good standing with the government and his obvious desire to secure the continued existence of the church were impressive, and they were prepared to give him and the Movement their support. But there were many Christians who failed to discover in Mr. Wu the authentic characteristics of the true Christian—a devotion to the Word of God and a prayerful reliance on the Spirit of God—and they were deeply suspicious of the Movement and its activities.

There were six vice-presidents of the Three-Self Movement—an Anglican bishop, the Secretary of the Church of Christ in China, and two men and one woman engaged in theological education.[4]

Of these, the Rev. Marcus Cheng, President of the Chungking Theological Seminary, is well known in evangelical circles in America, Great Britain, and Sweden. It is significant that his son had for a long time been a Communist, and it was apparent during his last visit to America and Europe that Mr. Cheng's sympathies were also toward the Left. In the autumn of 1953 the Rev. Gustav Nystrom of the Swedish Missionary Society visited Peking as the official interpreter for Secretary Dag Hammerskjold

---

[4]Bishop Robin Chen, Chairman of the Anglican House of Bishops; Miss Wu Yi-feng, formerly president of the Ginling Women's Seminary, Nanking; Rev. Marcus Cheng, President of the Chungking Theological Seminary; Rev. Tsui Hsien-hsiang, Executive Secretary of the Church of Christ in China; and Rev. Ting Yu-chang, vice-president of Ginling Seminary, Nanking.

of the United Nations. He specially asked Mr. Chou En-
lai, the Premier, if he could meet his old friend Marcus
Cheng. The result was a four hour meeting in the Peking
Hotel. Mr. Nystrom described Mr. Cheng as "a convinc-
ing and acceptable Communist" and Mr. Cheng himself,
in an article entitled, "The Stages of Change in My Political Thinking," wrote:

> I finally awakened. Only Marx and Lenin and the
> science of revolution are the tools which will set hu-
> manity free. . . . From the heart I can sincerely say that
> I fervently love Communism and accept the teaching of
> the Communist Party and the teachings of Mao Tze-
> tung . . . even as I accept astronomy and the fact that
> the earth is round or the statements in the Bible that
> the sun rises in the east and sets in the west. . . . There
> are some Christians who, when they hear of my change
> of thinking and that I have joined the Communist
> Party, and further that I have joined the Soviet-Russian
> Fellowship, think it very strange. Others freely abuse
> me. . . . Going through the Studies and seeing the facts
> has caused me to hate and oppose and despise America
> more than ever and through the same power be drawn
> closer to the pure, loving friendship of Russia.

During the summer of 1951, Marcus Cheng, who claims
to have exchanged blessings with the Pope at the Vatican
in 1949, was given the task of trying to unite Chinese
Roman Catholics and Protestants into one Reform Church!
Apparently, without marked success! Subsequently, however, the Chinese government did succeed in creating a
movement within the Roman Catholic Church correspond-
ing to the Protestant Three-Self Patriotic Movement. Joint
study groups for Protestants and Roman Catholics are a
common feature today. Marcus Cheng, like Mr. Wu, was
given a place in the P.P.C.C., where he has from time to
time made speeches before the highest in the land and

therefore has become a well-known figure on the Chinese scene.

An advanced liberal and a conservative evangelical! Who could have suspected that such strange "bedfellows" would ever be found together? But, in a predominantly liberal committee, it served the cause of the Three-Self Movement well to include such a prominent evangelical leader as Marcus Cheng. To some extent it disarmed the suspicions of evangelical churches everywhere and made them more inclined to throw in their lot with the Movement.

Frequent reference has been made to the official organ of the Movement—*Heavenly Wind (Tien Feng)*. Several other Christian papers have been in circulation, but it is *Heavenly Wind* that has the official support of the government and the Three-Self Movement. An analysis of the contents of this paper over several months in 1958 reveals that 48 per cent was secular propaganda for Communism; 36 per cent was religious propaganda with a political content; 12 per cent consisted of sound devotional and Bible study articles; 1 per cent of non-political church news, and 3 per cent of editorial comment. This shows that 84 per cent of the contents was either political or semi-political. This is probably typical of this magazine from the time the Communists gained control. It reflects the fact that the main interests of the Three-Self Movement have always been political and that the main purpose of the magazine, as of the Movement, is political—namely, to be an instrument of propaganda in favor of world-Communism. This fact was hidden from the unhappy people involved, and they continued to believe that in the Three-Self Movement lay the best home for the Christian church.

Chapter 5

ACCUSER OF THE BRETHREN

ONE OF THE DARKEST and most tragic features of the church's history under Communism has been the non-stop accusation campaign. Imagine a man having to continue his pastoral work with the walls of the church covered with hundreds of accusations against him! His sister committed suicide under the strain.

Again, imagine a man being ordered to prepare a self-denunciation. Draft after draft is rejected as inadequate. The man worked night and day at revising the text and in scrutinizing his past life to find anything of possible interest to his Communist masters which might be included.

Is it any wonder that there have been mental breakdowns and suicides? The constant fear of being subjected to the process has weighed heavily on the mind. And the process itself has involved intolerable mental strain and anxiety for all concerned. Anything further from the spirit of fervent love, which should mark the Christian fellowship, is hard to imagine. How Christians could have been maneuvered into involvement in the accusation of their Christian brethren is one of the mysteries hard for those outside China to understand. The psychological principle involved is perhaps the Devil's parody of James 5:16: "Confess your faults one to another, and pray for one another."

The first accusation campaign was launched during the April 1951 conference in Peking at which the Three-Self

Reform Movement was inaugurated. At that conference the chairman was an atheist official. Foreign missionaries were by that time pouring out of China and the first stage in the government program for the church was being accomplished. It was necessary then to deal with all their sympathizers—those who supposedly were infected with "imperialist poison" and harbored reactionary, anti-party sentiments. The term "imperialist" conveniently covered a variety of things—everything, in fact, that the Communists disliked about the church and Christians: their doctrines, their friendship with missionaries, their anti-atheist convictions, and their dislike of the Communist theory. Several years of investigation had by then revealed who were the "counterrevolutionaries," the "pro-imperialists," the "reactionaries," and the "corrupt elements" within the churches. The time had come to begin to root them out. Fear was the weapon used.

It was at Peking, therefore, that the prototype of church "accusation meetings" throughout China was staged. The two men singled out for attack were Ku Jen-en, an evangelist, and Bishop Chen Wen-yuan, a Methodist. A fellow Methodist bishop, Kiang Chang-chuan, accused Bishop Chen of being a spy for the Americans. Mr. Ku was accused of various crimes for which this conference of Christians actually demanded the death penalty! In the end both men were imprisoned. The conference was also addressed by a well-known Communist writer and anthropologist, Kuo Mo-jo, and by the Government Chief of Information, Lu Ting-yi, who very bluntly told his audience that the church would have to carry out Communist policies if they wanted to survive.

At that time the whole country was in the grip of fear. A wave of arrests and mass trials was sweeping over it. April 27 was a Black Saturday when in the early hours of the morning there were 16,000 arrests in Shanghai alone.

The insistence on wholesale self-criticism drove many to take their lives. One such was Mr. T. H. Sun, the editor of *Christian Farmer*.

Against this background the Three-Self Movement, which had set up its headquarters in the National Y.M.C.A. in Shanghai, planned to hold a huge accusation meeting on Sunday, June 10, in the Canidrome Stadium. Representatives of all the churches and Christian organizations in Shanghai were to "expose the crimes of the American imperialists in using the Christian church for its aggression in China." Intense and elaborate preparations went on for weeks. Every detail was rehearsed each Thursday as carefully as actors rehearse a play under an exacting producer. Even the "spontaneous reactions" of the audience were rehearsed to the point of perfection!

There were ten chief actors or "accusers," representing religious groups with a nation-wide following. These had laboriously prepared, with official help, a half-hour speech. Weeks of research had been necessary to insure that the "facts" were sufficiently damning and the scripts written in language sufficiently violent. Miss Mary Liu,[1] of the Christian Literature Society staff and editor of *Women's Messenger* and *Happy Childhood* had been selected by the government to represent her society, but she had adamantly refused to accuse her missionary colleagues. Consequently her draft speech was regarded as unsatisfactory, and Mr. Y. T. Wu read the accusation speech instead.

A vast synchronized publicity was focused on the meeting, which had sensational advance publicity. The eyes of Shanghai and also of the nation were on this first large-scale accusation meeting for the churches. The day dawned; it was as hot and humid as Shanghai can be in June. Each organization sent its participants in a group with its own leader, and everyone had a name card pinned

[1]*The Story of Mary Liu,* by Edward Hunter, Hodder & Stoughton.

to his clothes. The groups were instructed where to stand outside the stadium, where and when to enter. The groups assembled at half-past eleven. An hour and a half later they entered the stadium. It was blazing hot and a four-hour meeting lay ahead of them. Churchgoers were given seats in the covered stand, but employees of Christian organizations had to stand in the open on the scorching concrete. First-aid squads were kept busy helping those who fainted, while the speeches went on and on with their fantastic statements against the missionaries, made with faces contorted in feigned hate and calculated indignation. At six o'clock in the evening the crowd dispersed.

The next morning the daily papers carried lengthy accounts of the proceedings, which had obviously been designed to inflict a severe loss of face on America, the missionary movement, and the Christian church itself. What did it matter if all the participants knew well that the whole thing was a huge piece of acting? Those who would read the accounts of the meeting throughout the country would not know that and would believe what they read.

After this, the accusation campaign got into full swing. It was skillfully co-ordinated in every possible way—within each denomination and between the denominations, nationally and locally. The officials responsible were carefully selected, and Bishop Robin Chen was in charge. As soon as any church or denomination had passed through the purging process of self-criticism and accusation, it could then apply to the Three-Self Movement to set up a "reform church." It was anticipated that the campaign would go on for years, and go on it did!

The first denomination to qualify for the new status was the Seventh Day Adventist Church. A rally was held in early October in the Allen Memorial Church in the Hong-kew area of Shanghai, attended by representatives of all the city churches. The same carefully staged performance took place. There were fierce and passionate accusations of leading Adventists and the Christian audience whipped itself into a pagan fury as they again demanded the death of three of the accused! The din was like that of a football crowd. At the close, Mr. Y. T. Wu made a final speech congratulating the meeting on a "forceful demonstration." Later he declared that through the process of accusation and self-criticism the Adventist Church had undergone a rebirth and was therefore qualified to become a "reform church." The Adventists thereafter reorganized themselves as the first denominational branch of the Three-Self Committee. Accusation meetings then followed in every Adventist church throughout the country.

The procedure was the same everywhere. The Three-Self Movement, under the guidance of the local Communist cadres, selected the targets—the pastor or a leading church worker, or perhaps both. A church meeting was called at which all members had to be present. The accused was named, previously selected colleagues or church members, properly briefed, arose in turn to enumerate the alleged crimes committed by the accused person and other persons such as missionaries who had once been connected with the church. For this purpose, the past record of the accused, his relationship with missionaries, his written articles and public statements had been carefully investigated. Taken out of context, the spoken or written word and even the most innocent actions could become criminal in the hands of unscrupulous people. The outcome was always the same—a verdict of guilty, and the demand for the punishment of the offender. The government then took over and meted out hard labor, prison, and even death. The individual was often expelled from his church and suffered defamation of character and public disgrace.

Christian publishers in Shanghai had been in trouble even before the Peking Conference. At a conference in

March in Peking, a merger was decided upon between the Christian Literature Society, the Association Press (Y.M.C.A.) , the China Sunday School Union, and the Baptist Press. Mr. Y. T. Wu was to be the director. It was not long before the publications of these societies were purged of all literature which the Communists considered unsatisfactory. The result was that only twenty per cent of their stocks remained—the rest was destroyed.

Mr. T. Y. Hu was appointed to represent the Christian Literature Society at the Peking Conference and on his return he reported to the Society the necessity for a thoroughgoing reform. Normal work ceased, and preparations for accusations and self-criticism took its place. The news of Mr. T. H. Sun's suicide under fearful mental pressure shocked all his colleagues. In the weeks that followed Miss Mary Liu was often tempted to follow his example. Because of her refusal to accuse her former missionary colleagues and friends at the Canidrome meeting, she was soundly berated at the Religious Affairs Bureau as a "backward element." To atone for her failure and achieve a "rebirth," she was to prepare a self-criticism for a special meeting called for August 4, "to expose the crimes of American missionaries in using Christian publications to promote cultural aggression in China."

Repeated and pressing attempts were again made to get Mary Liu to make fantastic charges against her missionary friends. The records of twenty years were combed, and past employees of the Society were summoned to a meeting to help provide material. Lengthy and wearisome discussions induce that mental and physical fatigue in which the victim loses control over the mind. The result was a full self-criticism containing imputations that she had been harmed, exploited, and "poisoned" by her foreign friends.

At the end of July, Miss Liu and a colleague (Mr. Z. K. Zia) were summoned to the Religious Affairs Bureau to receive final instructions from three prominent Christians, including a bishop, on how to deliver their self-criticisms and accusations. As this was the first case of a public self-criticism to be publicized in any religious organization in China, arrangements for the meeting were meticulously made.

August 4 was unbearably hot. The four hundred representatives of the churches of Shanghai, the Religious Affairs Bureau, the police, and the press were provided on arrival with printed programs containing a list of slogans and with space where comments on the proceedings could be recorded.

Dr. Chang of the Council of Christian Publishers spoke first. Mr. Chester Miao, formerly of the China Bible House, spoke next, accusing the Rev. Ralph A. Mortensen of the American Bible Society. Mary Liu's colleague briefly confessed the "errors of his past ideas," and last came Miss Liu with her confession of a long list of crimes.

At the conclusion of the performance, Mr. Y. T. Wu and others came forward to congratulate her on her "rebirth." Not long afterward, Miss Liu resigned from the Christian Literature Society and was eventually able to reach Hong Kong—and freedom.

The same tragic farce was being enacted everywhere. After the Peking Conference, Mr. Li Sao-tuan, Secretary of the China Bible House in Hankow, was accused before a full meeting in a theater by fourteen of his own church members and handed over to the police for punishment.

In Nanking, the Rev. Yang Shao-tang (David Yang) was accused in a public meeting by some of his own converts and his former Bible Seminary students and colleagues. As a result he was expelled from his church.

In some cases children accused their own parents. In Peking, for example, the twenty-six-year old daughter of

Dr. Li Chih-wei, President of Yenching University, mounted the platform and publicly denounced her father.

In southwest China, when Archdeacon James Fu was accused by his own sons, he committed suicide.

In Kaifeng, an Anglican minister, the Rev. Tung Ling-ku, was accused repeatedly by twelve of his own church leaders and handed over to the police because of his outspoken opposition to the "accusation campaign." When he went to prison he left a wife and six children behind. It is probable that thousands of Christians suffered similarly at that time.

The religious press heartily supported the campaign. Obloquy was heaped on each of the more prominent victims. The campaigns were given scriptural justification in many articles contributed to *Heavenly Wind* on the subject. Did not the Bible provide precedents? Was it not Jesus Himself who was the first accuser when He vehemently accused and denounced the Pharisees? And should not we therefore equally accuse the corrupt elements within the church? In this way Biblical sanction was speciously given to this fearful campaign.

Christians who have never lived under the tremendous psychological pressures of a Communist state cannot be expected to understand how Christians could in this way betray their Lord and the Christian fellowship by providing the adversaries of the church with devilish and damaging ammunition to fire at them. Wherever Christians are faced by a common spiritual foe they cannot afford to criticize one another, much less make a public example of them. If there are wrongs within the fellowship, the Bible provides instructions for dealing with them. But to the enemy without, the Apostle Paul defines the proper attiude: "Stand fast in one spirit, with one mind striving together for the faith of the gospel; And in nothing terrified by your adversaries" (Phil. 1:27-28).

That the church failed in these respects and that the Three-Self Movement deliberately sponsored such a non-Christian campaign is further irrefutable evidence that it was not a free agent but the tool of the government. In a society which has always held family loyalty very high, and in a country where the church has experienced much of Christian fellowship, what other explanation can there be of the Communist success in dividing brethren by accusation of one another?

Chapter 6

MR. VALIANT-FOR-TRUTH

WHAT DID YOU FIND OUT about Mr. Wang Ming-tao?"
members of the Friends Mission to China were
asked in London after giving a rather glowing report of the
state of the church there. One of the delegates regretted Mr.
Wang's imprisonment, but took the view that he had
brought trouble on himself by his fundamentalist outlook
and opposition to the Three-Self Patriotic Movement and
by his unwise political attitudes. This was precisely the
Communist viewpoint and evidently this particular Mission had accepted it as the truth.

Although converted through the work of a foreign mission and educated in a Peking mission school, Mr. Wang
Ming-tao owes as little as any Christian worker to foreign
missions. He was not trained theologically by them, nor
was he ordained by them, and consequently had never
been in their employ at any time. Indeed, few Chinese
Christian leaders have been so independent of foreign
missions, or have been so severely critical of their mistakes
and shortcomings as Mr. Wang. At the same time few have
shown such personal regard and Christian love for individual missionaries. Mr. Wang has always been vigorously
independent and has followed a rigidly Biblical pathway
without straying, as some other independent Chinese
leaders have done, into extremes of doctrines and practice.
Through his eloquent Biblical sermons in his church in
East Peking, through his extensive convention ministry,
and through his widely read writings he has made an im-

pressive contribution to the spiritual life of the Chinese church. He was moreover a man of unimpeachable character and blameless record.

In an autobiography published in 1950 on his fiftieth birthday, Mr. Wang traced God's dealings with him and gave details of the firm and courageous stand he took during the Japanese occupation. The Japanese, like the Communists, had been anxious to have a unified church embracing everybody and officially sponsored by the puppet Chinese government. There were persistent attempts to persuade Mr. Wang to associate his church with this union. Time after time he faced death rather than compromise. He even purchased his coffin and kept it at home in readiness for the day when he might have to die for his stand! God honored his faithfulness and despite threats and flattery he weathered the storm and maintained the independence of his congregation throughout the Sino-Japanese war.

Mr. Wang Ming-tao was just as uncompromising where Biblical truth was concerned. He was a bitter foe of the liberal theology which has undermined the church's testimony to the world by depriving it of the voice of authority. He frequently named those who belittled the Scriptures or the Christ of the Scriptures. It was doubtless unfortunate for Mr. Wang, though by no means a coincidence, that these men were among those who came to prominence in the Three-Self Movement and who eventually brought about his downfall.

Wang Ming-tao was the chief thorn in the side of the Three-Self Movement because he represented all that they opposed. He, above everyone else, stood in the way of their attaining their goal of a united church. And very naturally he became the main target for their attacks. If they could break down his resistance, then the back of all resistance in the Chinese church would be broken. Through Mr.

Wang's notable stand, he has become to the world a symbol of courageous resistance to the Communist tyranny and its pathetic puppets.

Mr. Y. T. Wu had often expressed his own condemnation of the conservative evangelical section of the Christian church: derisively he called it the "spiritual party." Once he said, "They regard themselves as being above politics, they have a 'holier-than-thou' attitude, they twist the Scriptures, they proclaim the superiority of the church above the government, they oppose Russia, Communism and the People, and they spread poisonous thinking." Thus from the first the main target of Three-Self opposition within the church was the evangelical section, personified by Mr. Wang Ming-tao.

Following the Communist capture of Peking, Mr. Wang continued to preach and teach as usual. Each summer he was a welcome speaker at the Peking student conferences which had been an annual event since 1946. The students loved him and flocked to his church. He continued also to publish his magazine, *Spiritual Food Quarterly*, and from time to time other publications of moment. There was no question of his shrinking from what lay before him as he deliberately set himself to maintain an uncompromising testimony in the midst of a compromising church. In the November 1951 issue of *Spiritual Food Quarterly* which followed the inauguration of the Three-Self Reform Movement, he wrote:

> At that time [viz., 1927, when he first published the magazine] I already knew that if in this present time I faithfully proclaimed the Word of God—rebuking the sins, the evils, and the doctrine-destroying teachings in the corrupted, nominal church—I should surely meet the opposition and persecution which met Martin Luther. But there was one slight difference. The church today is not faced with as great an opponent as that

power of the Roman church in the sixteenth century.
Therefore it could not with authority and power crush
one who faithfully preached the Word, though it would
unwillingly see men rise up to point out the depths of
corruption and doctrine denial to which that church
had sunk. Under these conditions the one who faithfully preaches the Word of God cannot but expect to meet
opposition from some leaders in the church and from
"Christians" who are spiritually dead, in the form of
malicious slander and abuse. I know that this will come
to pass. I am prepared to meet it. I covet the courage
and faithfulness of Martin Luther. Therefore I again
in this issue (November 1951) reprint his prayer:

"Almighty and Eternal God! How fearful is this
world as it bares its great teeth to eat one up! How
weak is my heart as it rests in Thee! My God, help me
that I may thwart all the wisdom of this world . . . I
have no quarrel with the rulers of this world. I, myself,
would wish to spend my days in happiness and peace!
. . . But the affairs of this day are for Thy cause! Thy
cause is just and righteous and everlasting! . . . I pray
Thee for the sake of Thy beloved Son, Jesus Christ, be
at my side! He is my Fortress, He is my Shield, He also
is my Defense. Now I am prepared and ready. Ready
to give my life for Thy truth—weak and helpless as a
lamb. Though the world be filled with devils, though
for punishment they put me in the stocks and tear me
to pieces or cut me up, yes, though they burn me to
ashes, yet is my life with Thee. . . . Amen! O God, I
pray Thee, help me! Amen!"

In this spirit, Mr. Wang continued to preach separation
from the world and its spirit and to proclaim the separate
and holy character of the church in the world. "Love not
the world" was a favorite theme. The church cannot come
to terms with the world without compromise, he declared.
By implication, a church which was entangled in the affairs
of this world, its politics and policies, a church which had

become the meek servant of an atheist government, had ceased to function as the true church of Jesus Christ. Such preaching and writing became increasingly embarrassing to the leaders of the Three-Self Movement and a major hindrance to progress in the task assigned to them by the government. But to Mr. Wang was given the privilege of clarifying the real issues which were basically theological and doctrinal.

Early in 1954 there were rumors that Mr. Wang Ming-tao had been executed, the report apparently originating from a Radio Peking broadcast. The facts behind this report are that in the spring of that year the Three-Self Movement sent out an order to all the churches and Christian organizations in Peking to appoint delegates to attend a meeting at which Mr. Wang was to be accused. The charges against him were (1) he had not shown sympathy with the government; (2) he had not taken part in the Three-Self Reform Movement; and (3) his preaching was very individualistic and its purpose not clear. He was declared to be a danger to the whole Christian cause. There was great excitement at the meeting, with many people raising their voices at the same time. Mr. Wang himself sat quietly on the platform, his eyes fixed on the ceiling, never uttering a word. Some people tried to leave early in protest but were prevented from doing so. Following the accusations, the demand was voiced that he should suffer the death penalty or at least be sent to prison. But not more than a quarter of those present gave their assent to these proposals. The others sat silent—some weeping. No punishment was decreed! It was this demand for Wang Ming-tao's death that undoubtedly lay behind the rumor of his execution.

Several days after the meeting, the evangelical student organization in Peking started an "Oppose the Persecution of Wang Ming-tao" campaign. Many of the students were members of Mr. Wang's church. The campaign spread rapidly and was supported by other Peking churches and organizations. From Peking it spread to Tientsin and Shanghai and so the agitation was publicized all over China. For some weeks after the accusation meeting, Mr. Wang, who had recently been in poor health, did not preach publicly but confined himself to leading prayer meetings in his own home and to writing and personal interviews. By this time no printer dared to print his magazine, and he himself used to set up his own type and print his own books and magazines—a laborious task which kept him working often until after midnight.

When he resumed preaching it was to larger crowds than ever. In January 1955 he held the largest attended winter evangelistic meetings he had ever conducted, and they resulted in many conversions. The two weeks of meetings in his church in July again attracted a record attendance. In August Mr. and Mrs. Wang were given the opportunity of taking a two-week vacation at the seashore resort of Peitaiho, where he continued to do a little writing. In the autumn, further issues of the magazine and a number of reprints were set up in type by his own hands: *Truth or Poison?* and *Loyalty to God Without Respect of Person.* Many of these articles were strongly polemic and openly critical of the Three-Self Movement—especially of those evangelicals who had given it their support. Doubtless with Wang Ming-tao in mind, Professor Hsieh Shou-ling, of the faculty of Yenching School of Theology, published the text of a sermon on the *Magnificat* in a church magazine. One paragraph of this sermon read as follows:

> The Christian church in its nature, like the Jewish faith, holds a religious principle which divides mankind into two groups—those within the church and those outside the church. . . . Likewise today there are those within the church who are unwilling to disregard

this type of religious prejudice. They continue to preach the two positions or standpoints. They do not realize that today there is only one position, namely, that of the People. . . . Whoever are with the People, they are God's chosen, the children of God. Whoever stands in opposition to the People, whether they stand within the church or without, they are the enemies of God. They are the children of the devil. Their end is eventually destruction.

On another occasion Professor Hsieh analyzed the thinking of Mr. Wang and the reasons why he and his kind would not associate with the progressive Christians, and ended with a threat that such an attitude could not be tolerated.

It is clear that Wang Ming-tao did not accept the official view that all missionary work from beginning to end had been one vast imperialist plot. In his article in *Spiritual Food Quarterly* entitled "Truth or Poison?" Mr. Wang had carefully collected statements made by the leaders of the Three-Self Movement to the effect that (1) the poison of thought, propagated by the imperialists, had obscured the true light of the Gospel; (2) Christianity had been used as an instrument of imperialist aggression; (3) for the past hundred years the imperialists had made use of the missionary enterprise to pervert Biblical teaching and to disseminate poison in the realm of thought; (4) the basic cause of the bad relations of ministers with the Chinese people was the "imperialist poison" which had done such harm to the church; (5) the imperialists, taking advantage of missionary work for aggressive purposes, had deliberately perverted the truth in Christ in order to spread this poison in disguise.

Mr. Wang had no brief for foreign missions as such, but he was passionately interested in truth. And he went on to describe the serious and confusing effect such assertions had had on the minds of many Christians who had been tempted to wonder whether what they had learned from the missionaries was really truth or poison. He then blamed the Three-Self Movement for not being more explicit about the alleged "poisonous doctrines," but went on to say that by careful research he had been able to identify them. They were these: (a) emphasizing the distinction between Christians and atheists; (b) advocating the principle, "Be not unequally yoked together with unbelievers"; (c) and attacking other Christians with differing beliefs. Having isolated these so-called poisons, Mr. Wang proceeded to demonstrate that they were essentially scriptural and he seriously warned those who tried to frighten Christians into giving up these doctrines. He analyzed the reasons for denouncing these truths as an endeavor to assist their atheist masters in the destruction of the true Gospel. Communists knew that the Gospel could not be destroyed by open persecution or crushed by government edict, so their policy was to promote all kinds of anti-Christian propaganda within the church in an endeavor to undermine the basic beliefs of Christians. The Communist government was not afraid of a church in which there were only the outward form and ritual without any inner life or convictions, and he added—prophetically and significantly in the light of later events: *"If the Church should ever be reduced to such a state, though there were Sunday services and other religious formalities, she would in fact have already been liquidated."* Those who energetically promoted the "imperialist poison" propaganda were just as surely betraying their own church as Judas did his Lord. Mr. Wang's concluding words are memorable and must be quoted at length:

In conclusion, a word to the saints. In the Scriptures there is nothing but the pure truth of God, without any "imperialist poison." . . . We must go on believing and preaching it. Nobody can interfere with us, and nobody can forbid us to do this. We are ready to pay any price to preserve the Word of God and we are equally willing to sacrifice anything in order to preach the Word of God. . . . Dear brothers and sisters, let us be strong through the mighty power of the Lord! Let us profess our faith with courage and spread the Gospel with zeal! Let us be prepared to be faithful to the Lord at any cost! Our God is almighty and He will keep all those who are faithful to Him. Our Lord is the Lord of victory, who will lead us from victory unto victory. Now is the time for us to stand up and fight for His holy name, for His Gospel, and for His church. Don't be cowards! Don't be weary! Don't give way! Don't compromise! The battle is indeed furious and the battlefield certainly full of dangers, but God's glory will be manifest there. He will honor them who honor Him. He will glorify those who glorify Him. Hark! The trumpet has been blown! Look, the victory is in sight! My dear brothers and sisters, let us follow in the steps of the Lord and, holding aloft His banner, go forward courageously for His Gospel's sake.

In this pamphlet, Mr. Wang had flung down the gauntlet to the Three-Self leaders—and they accepted the challenge. This powerful opposition to the Movement could not be allowed to go on, affecting as it did the attitude toward the Movement of many Christians and churches throughout China.

In May 1955, the Three-Self Movement held its fourth annual conference in Peking attended by six hundred delegates from all branches of the Christian church. The leaders decided to make one last effort to win Mr. Wang Mingtao over. Six of its most prominent men called to see Mr. Wang at his home but he refused to meet them. The following month, the Three-Self Movement leaders ordered accusation meetings to be held all over China against Mr. Wang. It happened that at the same time Mr. Hu Feng, a well-known Communist writer, had been expelled from the Party, and Mr. Wang Ming-tao shared with him the headlines in both the secular and the religious press. Every kind of opprobrium was heaped upon him. He name became notorious throughout the whole of China. *Heavenly Wind* featured reports of all the church accusation meetings at which he had been execrated.

On July 31 a special article appeared in *Heavenly Wind:* "Strengthen Unity, Recognize Realities!—a Summons from the Three-Self Patriotic Movement." This was an open attack on Mr. Wang Ming-tao. All his "crimes" were listed, and the writer had this to say:

> We were early aware that there were groups like Wang Ming-tao's, with their stubborn errors. In a changing time, they are completely unchangeable. With this attitude they are destroying our Three-Self Patriotic Movement. The greater our victory, the greater their activity to destroy. In his relationship to the New China, Wang Ming-tao has no feeling for the People for he has a heart of lead. The benefits of the day are shrouded in darkness. This attitude of political hatred naturally destroys the "Oppose Imperialism—Love One's Country" Movement.

On July 25, forty-nine responsible leaders from all churches and institutions met in Hankow as the Wuhan Leadership Studies Group to accuse Mr. Wang. The meeting lasted all day but only twenty-three had time to speak. One after another erstwhile friends and lifelong enemies poured out their accusations against Mr. Wang, including a fair proportion of men with an evangelical background. Finally they drew up a statement ending with these words: "We hope that he will recognize his errors and that he will 'rein in before he comes to the precipice,' and not adhere to error, but eternally take his stand with the people."

The nationwide publicity for the case of Wang Ming-tao had set the stage for what was to come. The storm was about to break over the head of God's servant, and he knew it. On August 7, fully realizing that his arrest might be expected at any time, he preached what proved to be his last sermon, "The Son of man is betrayed into the hands of sinners." This was a pointed reference to the great betrayal of Christ by the official church in China. And after the sermon he distributed copies of a new pamphlet entitled, "We, Because of Our Faith . . . ," his own manifesto to the world as to the issues at stake. Present events, he maintained, were but a continuation of the familiar old conflict between those who accepted the authority of the Word of God and lived in obedience to its teaching, and unbelievers who minimized the authority of Holy Scripture and set themselves up as its critics. His conclusion was:

> We wish earnestly to say this: we will not be united with unbelievers, and we will never join any of their organizations. We are united with all true Christians in their service to the Lord—deeply united in the Spirit. But we ought not to be forced to join together in a formal organization. We do not find this commanded or suggested in the Bible. Our behavior is according to faith. Whatever is in keeping with the truth of the Word, we accept and keep. What the Bible does not command we reject. We shall make whatever sacrifice is required of us in being faithful to God. The twisting of the Word and the consequent falsehoods cannot intimidate us! Men are free to say what they like, but Christian truth never changes! Believers see this clearly. Regardless of how others may twist the truth and slander us, *we because of our faith shall remain steadfast!*

Mr. Wang did not have to wait long. That night (at about one o'clock) there was a summons at the gate from the police. Mr. and Mrs. Wang were roused from sleep and ordered to dress hurriedly. They were bound with ropes and taken off to jail. Eighteen young Christians of college and university age who were regular members of Mr. Wang's church were arrested at the same time. All were charged with resistance to the government, though Mr. Wang had never spoken a single word of criticism of the government as such. His resistance had been to the Three-Self Movement.

A letter written from Peking on the day of the arrests said: "Praise God, they love their Lord! They are pleasing in His sight! Within the nation the spirited warfare against the evangelical elements of the church has risen to an unprecedented intensity in the arrest of the faithful servants of the Lord Jesus Christ, Mr. and Mrs. Wang Ming-tao, his helpers and deacons. Peking has other servants of the Lord and believers who are also prepared to meet persecution." The writer appropriately quoted Luke 23:2: "They began to accuse him, saying, We found this fellow perverting the nation, and forbidding to give tribute to Caesar." So was history repeating itself, for the issues which faced the early church were the same as those facing the church in a Communist society today.

Mr. Wang's place in the pulpit was taken by one of his colleagues, but not long after he too was arrested and imprisoned. The church was closed and the doors sealed. Those were not the only arrests during that tragic late summer and autumn. During September and October there was a wave of similar arrests throughout China—in the church and outside it.

Wang Ming-tao was originally sentenced to fifteen years imprisonment. However, after only thirteen months in prison he was released on September 30, 1956. During his time in prison he always had two men with him in his cell and they subjected him to incessant discussion, argument, and debate, using the well-known psychological pressures at which the Communist world is so expert. On his release he appeared physically well. At a public meeting in Peking called to welcome his release, Mr. Wang read a prepared statement entitled "Self Examination." It opened with the words, "I am a person guilty of anti-revolutionary deeds. I am obliged to the patient education of the government which made me realize my own mistakes, and yet the government dealt with me genuinely and has delivered me from the deep gulf of crime. . . . Concerning my criminal deeds, I have already confessed to the government the whole matter frankly." The address was of course published in full in *Heavenly Wind*, with the following editorial note:

Mr. Wang Ming-tao, pastor of the Christian Tabernacle in Peking, through his counterrevolutionary activities since Liberation, stirred up the whole Chinese church against him. . . . During the last year, under government tuition, Mr. Wang's thoughts and understanding have undergone a great change and he has seen his faults and brought his sin to light. On September 30 he made his public confession before a large meeting of the delegates of the Three-Self Movement. In the above reported speech, Mr. Wang does not enumerate all his crimes, though he did this to the government. But he confesses how his contact with western imperialists over many years had affected him. He denounced the old Wang Ming-tao as a counterrevolutionary. We thank the government for their leniency with him considering his crimes. But if we honestly confess our sins, they will certainly be forgiven (Proverbs 28:13) ; so we hope all fellow Christians will lovingly help Wang Ming-tao to continue his awakening and identify himself more completely with the people. And we hope that Wang Ming-tao will make this confession a starting point from which to rid his mind completely of all imperialist poisons and so make up for all past errors. We welcome Wang Ming-tao to join us in the Christian patriotic anti-imperialism fellowship and in the zealous reconstruction of the Chinese church.

But Mr. Wang was in no mental condition to do any such thing. His body might appear to be normal, but his mind had been affected. He was unable to preach and it was soon clear that he was suffering a mental breakdown. He would go about like one demented, shouting, "I am Peter!" or at times, "I am Judas!" He was certainly unfit to preach, for he was undergoing the tortures of extreme depression and an accusing conscience, blaming himself that he had both betrayed and denied his Lord.

Other imprisoned Christians were released about the same time—in Shanghai as well as in Peking. As the Archbishop Mowll delegation from Australia was about to visit China, it may be that the release was intended to create a more favorable impression on the minds of the visiting clergy.

But it was not long before Mr. Wang was back in prison again. The time came when he and his wife decided to inform the authorities that the statement which was made on his release was not his own and did not in fact represent his true convictions. Thus Mr. Valiant-for-Truth at the last remained faithful to himself and to his God.

Chapter 7

TIME REDEEMED

THE ENMESHING OF THE CHURCHES in politics and their enslavement to a Communist ideal entrusted to the Three-Self Movement were promoted with the greatest vigor in the larger cities where the organization was strongest and most effective. Remote from the large cities, the Christian witness at first continued—if not normally, yet with infinitely greater freedom than in the great urban areas.

Among the Chinese missionary societies which came into being in the postwar years were the Back to Jerusalem Band, the Central Asia Spiritual Work Team, and the Christian Workers Mission. Individuals also heard the call of God to forsake the ease of the coastal cities for the rigors of missionary life in the west and northwest border regions.

At a July 1954 meeting in Tientsin, this report was given on the work of the Christian Workers Mission:

> In Inner Mongolia, it has been found very difficult to do anything but personal work; however, the workers there have endured much hardness on their long itinerations among the Mongols, both in the fierce heat of summer and in facing the bitter winds of winter. There have been several conversions among the nomads.
>
> At Hami, in Turkestan, the son of a Chinese father and a Russian mother is eagerly engaged in witnessing to Muslims with a converted Muslim companion. The church in this center is still active and, beside the Sunday services and Sunday school, holds a nightly cottage

meeting, a weekly prayer meeting, and a women's meeting. Evangelistic work for outsiders is very difficult. At Tihwa, capital of Sinkiang, there were nineteen baptisms at Easter, largely the result of meetings conducted last year by a Chinese evangelist and marked by deep conviction of sin and great interest in the Gospel. A Russian Christian is also active in the life of the church there. Several churches in the district which had been in low spiritual condition have been revived, and attendance at worship has greatly increased. The witness to both Muslims and tribespeople has been continuing, and a Muslim *ahung* (priest) and his wife have professed conversion. In southern Turkestan, a new church was planted in 1950 composed of Chinese, Russian, and Wei tribe believers. The leader was born in Russia and grew up in Turkestan, speaking three languages. To the north, on the Russian border, one of the Chinese missionaries, supporting himself by making confections, has been ministering to a congregation of about thirty Russian and Chinese Christians. They received a consignment of Russian Bibles, New Testaments, and other literature with great joy.

On the Tibetan frontier a China Bible Seminary graduate made Sining his center in 1950. From there he has made long journeys seeking fellowship with isolated believers, whom he found maintaining a vigorous witness for Christ locally: a shoemaker and a wool merchant in particular. The church in Sining has been through a dark period and many adherents have fallen away, but their places have been filled by others who have been truly born again of God's Spirit.

An enviable missionary report!

Reports from other sources showed that there was much cause for encouragement notwithstanding great difficulties. In Peking the annual student conference, started in 1947, had continued without a break and did so until 1955 at least, although the August 1955 conference met under the shadow of Wang Ming-tao's arrest and numbers were reduced from 300 to 100. The former Union Church for foreigners had become the center for a thriving student fellowship and witness, and all-night prayer meetings often preceded special consecration services. There were seven offshoots of this work throughout Mongolia and the northwest.

In Shanghai one large church arranged for a rota of sixty members to spend one hour daily, six at a time, from eight in the morning to six at night, in an unbroken chain of prayer. It is not surprising that 114 baptisms took place in that church in 1953. In the same year, too, a new church was opened in Shanghai and at special evangelistic meetings to celebrate the event about a hundred people stated that they wished to follow the Lord. At another church, on the other side of the river, many were reported to be seeking Christ and six had recently found Him. Students at one of the Shanghai medical colleges held special meetings in 1953 at which at least ten came to the Lord. In August 1954 nine hundred Christian students held a four-day conference in Shanghai. Some medical and technical graduates were putting in special requests to be sent to remote inland areas of China in order to witness for the Lord. Some ninety of these graduates met daily for Bible study and prayer early in the morning while awaiting their posting.

From a city in Yunnan came a report that there were six hundred people in the town and neighborhood linked with the church, and in spite of the long distances many had to travel, 150 people attended church every Sunday.

In 1955 the Christian Workers Mission again reported that the Chinese brother in Inner Mongolia had been continuing his travels and had found earlier converts going on well. Workers in this field reported that the doors were still wide open and that there was much to encourage.

Indeed, in the provincial capital, following special meetings for the Christians, there had been a small-scale revival resulting in the start of a nightly meeting for Bible study and prayer.

In Turkestan, the same mission reported that the work in the provincial capital was progressing and that nightly evangelistic services were being held in the church. A half-day Bible school was supervised by a converted Muslim and the students were being used of God. In other centers, too, there was much to encourage and fresh supplies of Christian literature had been thankfully received. At one place a Christian couple had opened what they named the Heavenly Glory Literature Shop. In another district of eighty thousand Mongols, many were turning to the Lord through the witness of another China Bible Seminary graduate. At Manass, where the leader was a Russian, God had visited the church in cleansing and quickening power.

On the Tibetan foothills, workers of the mission reported a full church on Sundays at Sining and further recent baptisms. In the country, village Christians were maintaining a testimony and strengthening one another's hands in the Lord. At one remote place a worker had found four Christian farmers who had had no contact with other Christians for five years but, in spite of persecution, they still confessed the name of Christ. Thirty miles farther on, he found one isolated Christian continuing faithful in prayer and Bible reading. Elsewhere he had found the Christians meeting twice daily—in the morning for Bible study and in the evening for prayer—and they were tithing their money for the Lord's work. Not far away he had been warmly received by a family of Tibetan Christians! At one Tibetan center, the little group of Christians had been revived and backsliders had been restored.

At the city in Kansu which had been the scene of the

sufferings of Arthur and Wilda Mathews,[1] Christians traveled long distances on Sundays to attend worship and there were usually seventy to eighty of them in church. There were still Christians at such places as Jade Gate and Golden Pagoda, but they sadly lacked pastoral care.

The Christian Workers Mission also had workers in southwest China and they, too, amid innumerable difficulties and with much ill health, were ministering to both tribal and Chinese congregations and were seeing men and women turn to God.

In March 1955 the Shanghai office of the Christian Workers Mission was suddenly closed and the editor of their publication, *The Holy Anointing*, and another member of the staff were arrested. There has been no news of them since, and no further reports of the Christian Workers Mission work.

In Shanghai the church with the remarkable prayer meeting reported a further two hundred baptisms; another church forty-two, while yet another had seventy-five additions to the church. A special Sunday school competition in 1954 in Shanghai had reached ten thousand boys and girls. In the province of Chekiang there were six hundred baptisms in 1955 and 1956; in one village where there had once been only three or four believers, there were in 1956 only three or four families who were *not* Christians.

A request for Chinese and tribal Scriptures had reached Shanghai from the southwest, from a man who had been a colporteur for over twenty years. This man was then in an area of seven large churches of tribal and Chinese believers, some of the congregations being as large as four or five hundred.

From the monastery town of Labrang in eastern Tibet there was news of a movement of the Spirit of God. For

---

[1] *Green Leaf in Drought-Time,* by Isobel Kuhn. Moody Press, cloth and paper.

years missionaries had witnessed there without seeing any results. Now, as the fruit of the witness of Chinese Christians, there was a group of baptized believers and men and women were freely turning to Christ.

In central China, too, there were extraordinary reports of increases in church membership. In one area where there has for long been a large and flourishing church, membership in one center increased by nearly two thousand in the years following the departure of the missionaries. In another mountainous area, the number of Christians increased in the same period from three hundred to three thousand. In Chekiang the increase in church membership in the Anglican church was said to be continuing at about the same rate as in the days before the Communist takeover.

The demand for Christian literature from all over China was very great, but where could it be obtained? There was a virtual ban on all Christian literature from outside China. In 1956 the major Christian bookshops entered into joint ownership with the Government. The result was that many evangelical books were discarded or sold to the Christian Book Room, which had been the chief source of supply for Christians all over China since the Communist takeover. Miss Helen Willis, the manager, was able to stay on until 1959 and supplied Christians all over China with evangelical books. Then her bookshop was closed and she herself was expelled from China on the charges of circulating Mr. Wang Ming-tao's books, helping reactionaries, and opposing the government program. Her sales locally had fluctuated with the changing climate of political feeling, but her trade with inland China had continued steady, and sales in 1958 exceeded all previous records.

The China Bible House continued to function in the face of great difficulties and was able to print fresh editions of Bibles from time to time as capital became available. But without foreign subsidies, Bibles had to be sold at cost price and were therefore beyond the pocket of many. As sales dropped, so capital dwindled, and the difficulties of producing and distributing the Scriptures increased. At one point the staff accepted a fifty per cent reduction in their salaries in order to keep going. Moreover, the Bible House was under constant fire from the authorities because of the "imperialistic conditions" prevailing. It was re-organized in 1955 and all the employees had to undergo two hours of political studies daily. Dr. Baen Lee, the General Secretary, had been arrested in 1954, but was released in 1956. Later he was arrested a second time and died during his imprisonment. His successor at the Bible House was soon in similar trouble.

In 1956 Dr. Chia Yu-ming's fifteen-volume commentary on the Bible began to appear. Others were working on a translation of the Bible Concordance by Strong, and a new translation of the Bible from the original text.

Reading these brief summaries, one rejoices that so many Christians were redeeming the time before even greater limitations were imposed on the preaching of the Gospel. If only freedom were restored, there is a faithful remnant in China ready to obey Christ's command to preach the Gospel to China's remotest bounds.

Chapter 8

THE GREAT DELUSION

T<small>HE CONDITIONS DESCRIBED</small> in the previous chapter were contemporary with the visits of different foreign Christians and delegations to China. Most of them returned with optimistic and favorable reports of what they had seen and heard in China. The authorities made sure that their guides were well briefed and that they should be given the opportunity to see the most favorable side of life in China under the Communists. Economically there was certainly much that was calculated to impress. But as far as the Christian church was concerned, appearances were deceptive.

In May 1954 a Norwegian delegation to China took back a letter to Norwegian Christians saying that there was true freedom of religion, that the churches were thriving and flourishing, and that they had not been asked to alter one iota of the historic Christian faith. This letter contained the kind of propaganda now expected of all patriotic Christians.

In January 1955 Dr. Nystrom had the interview already described with the Rev. Marcus Cheng and left China with a very favorable impression of the general church situation. Dr. Nystrom was an experienced observer but had to depend almost entirely on secondhand reports from official church spokesmen.

In June of the same year Bishop R. O. Hall of Hong Kong paid a brief visit to the mainland. In an interview with the Hong Kong press on his return he said, "The

35611

church in China is growing and vigorous, and there is no impediment to its work." To this the editor of one leading paper replied:

> There may be freedom for liturgical and religious practices, but the church must also be free to be the conscience of the state and of men. It must be free to voice its belief so that the secular community can be brought under the judgment of God. It must be free not only to praise God and adore Christ, but also to use Christian influence to correct the abuses of the social order and to protest its tyranny. It must be free to succor, help, and comfort all that are in danger, necessity, and tribulation. Unless the Christian church has the freedom to do these things, then it is free only as an "opiate of the masses," free only to be used as an instrument of the state.

In the autumn of 1955 a six-member Quaker mission paid their much-publicized visit to China. They were granted a two-hour interview with the Prime Minister, Mr. Chou En-lai. The *Manchester Guardian* of November 8, 1955, reported that the mission could confirm that the freedom of religious belief and worship guaranteed by the Constitution was in fact being granted. They described the life of the Christian church as flourishing, with large numbers of churches of all denominations in use in the cities visited and a good proportion of young people in the congregations. They said that the forebodings of Christians at the time of the revolution had been replaced by the feeling that it was a blessing in disguise. They reported that there were four main theological seminaries functioning in China. And they brought with them a beautifully prepared set of photographs of the leaders and activities of the church, all with English captions.

Later still, in 1956, following a visit to England to attend the preliminary committee of the Lambeth Conference by Bishop K. H. Ting, Archbishop H. W. K. Mowll of Sydney, accompanied by seven other bishops and clergy of the Anglican Church, visited China. It is significant that, unlike the Quaker mission, none of the members of this delegation could speak Chinese. The Archbishop visited his former diocese in West China and his detailed report provided solid evidence for the Archbishop's contention that the Anglican Church in China was not only functioning freely but was also a growing force. To which the General Secretary of the Australian Council of the World Council of Churches replied:

> The church in Communist China, or whatever is left of it, is now so fully a party to the plans and politics of the Government that it is actually an ally of that Government. It is playing its role in subverting men and women from the true Gospel of Jesus Christ. Its prophetic function is ended and Jesus Christ is not its King!

It was certainly very difficult in 1956 to discern the true state of affairs. Many well-intentioned Christians, like the members of the Quaker mission and the Australian Anglican mission, were prepared to give the Communist Government the benefit of the doubt and to interpret the comparative freedom of the Christians and the churches, the sort of freedom a canary enjoys within the bars of its cage, as evidence that the government was in fact tolerant to the Christian church and faithfully implementing its promise of religious freedom. In this they were deluded. Anyone familiar with the authoritative attitudes of doctrinaire Communists toward religion and who understands the subtlety of the Communist mind must know that the ultimate aim of the Communist Government in China or anywhere else is to reduce the church to impotence and to slavish obedience to the state; it is firmly believed that ultimately the Christian faith will die a natural death as the new generation grows up—nurtured in dialectical materialism and free from religious superstition. The Chinese Government can therefore, for the time being, afford to maintain the illusion that the church is free in order to disarm the prejudices of the Western world by an apparent and tactical tolerance toward religion. Only the "starry-eyed" really believe in Communist sincerity or that the apparent freedom is real freedom. The future was to reveal this ever more plainly.

Chapter 9

DISILLUSION

THE FIERCE ATTACK on Mr. Wang Ming-tao and the simultaneous wave of arrests of many evangelicals throughout the country undoubtedly shocked those whose cause Mr. Wang had so courageously championed. Resistance of the Wang Ming-tao kind to the Three-Self Movement no longer seemed possible. A Chinese pastor's daughter, writing to her parents outside China, said, "Do not try to contact me. We are walking the road from Gethsemane to Calvary!"

Heavenly Wind continued to carry attacks and articles against Wang Ming-tao throughout August and September 1955, and the nature of the articles makes it plain that there had been nationwide disapproval of Mr. Wang's sentence. To clinch things, therefore, in September church workers everywhere were required to express their personal condemnation of Wang Ming-tao and their approval of the action taken. One brave man who dared to quote Acts 5:38-39 (Gamaliel's words about fighting against God) was dismissed from his church. Not everyone had been cowed into unquestioning submission! But in the full list of names of the church leaders who had formally approved of Wang Ming-tao's punishment, published in the November *Heavenly Wind,* hardly any well-known name was missing.

Then, further to tighten the existing controls, the Three-Self Movement issued a decree in October declaring all Christian activities outside the jurisdiction of the Three-Self Movement to be illegal. Henceforth only activities directly sponsored by the official organization would be allowed. That meant that no private "cottage meetings" or gatherings to "break bread" in private homes might be held. The government Religious Affairs Bureau further conducted a house-to-house search of every Christian home and a careful examination of all Christian literature found there. Anything "pernicious," such as books by Wang Ming-tao, was confiscated. Some Christians became afraid to keep any Christian books in their homes.

Early in 1956 there began a major offensive against the Little Flock, whose leaders had adopted much the same attitude to the Three-Self Movement as Mr. Wang Ming-tao had. The Little Flock, a sobriquet derived from a quotation from John's Gospel in their hymnbook, is the name given by others to possibly the largest single group of Christians in China. They call their autonomous assemblies Christian Meeting Places, but they differ substantially from the Brethren Assemblies of the West. There are thousands of such assemblies throughout China, many of them having separated from older churches, but many also having been independent from their beginnings. The founder of this very influential movement was Mr. Nee To-sheng (Watchman Nee), a man with a brilliant mind, great ability, and unique qualities of leadership. Although the movement has been characterized by its exclusiveness and some erratic doctrinal emphases, it has been on the whole a movement true to the Word of God and maintaining very high spiritual standards.

Mr. Nee To-sheng used to own and manage a Christian pharmaceutical factory and had acquired extensive property in Fukien, his native province, for the use of his movement. During the Five-Anti campaign in 1952, Mr. Nee was imprisoned on charges of being a capitalist guilty of all five crimes; he is still serving a fifteen-year prison sentence in Shanghai. On January 21, 1956, the four elders who had continued the pastoral duties, together with some twenty-six other leaders in the Shanghai area, were arrested. On January 30, including both Little Flock members and pastors of other churches, 2,500 Christians were summoned to a mass denunciation meeting. The chairman of the Shanghai Religious Affairs Bureau (a Communist) was in the chair, and the main speech was made by the vice-mayor of Shanghai, another Communist.

The vice-mayor said that the arrests had not been made because of any opposition to the Three-Self Movement, though that in itself was a bad thing, but because the arrested were counterrevolutionaries. There was never any interference, he said, by the People's Government with religious belief, but the Government would not allow anyone to use religion to obstruct the socialist economy or to engage in counterrevolutionary activity. The Little Flock was not itself a counterrevolutionary organization, but there were counterrevolutionaries in it. These men had supported imperialism and the Nationalists, they had opposed popular movements, they had corrupted youth, they had sabotaged production and had acted licentiously. The last point was said to concern only Mr. Nee, who was accused of having seduced more than one hundred women! The struggle, said the mayor, had just begun, and they would not stop until they had rooted out every counterrevolutionary hidden within the Little Flock.

On February 2 over eight hundred people attended a Three-Self Movement meeting to assure the Government of their united support of the arrest and punishment of Watchman Nee and to pass a resolution to "purge out Nee To-sheng's reactionary and anti-revolutionary group." Speakers spoke of their "traitorous rebelling," their "dissipated and slanderous corruption," and their "abomination of everything in the New Society." The voices of well-known evangelicals once more joined with those of very different traditions to denounce Nee To-sheng. The Little Flock practice of pooling all private possessions came under heavy fire and nothing open to criticism seemed to escape attention. The daily press as well as the religious weeklies blazoned the accusations in their headlines and Watchman Nee was depicted to the world as an utterly corrupt criminal. The proceedings were reported in full in a publication called *Studies Reporter*.

All the members of the Little Flock in Shanghai were then divided into groups and put through an indoctrination course. Other evangelistic workers went around Shanghai acquainting the churches with the sins of the anti-revolutionary Nee To-sheng group. On April 15 the Little Flock church, having achieved a "rebirth," was completely reorganized and formally joined the Three-Self Movement. This was a major victory for the leaders of the Movement, but only achieved by strong Government support!

The next big event in the Three-Self Movement program was the Second National Conference of the Three-Self Patriotic Movement, which was convened in Peking March 15-23, 1956. The 269 delegates came from every province of China and were more completely representative of the churches and Christian organizations than ever before. There were some who had previously been under the "evil influence" of Wang Ming-tao and Nee To-sheng, who were now free to attend. The Little Flock itself was well represented, and their spokesmen disavowed their former leaders and wrong attitudes. There were four distinguished visitors from overseas present: Professor Joseph Hromadka of Czechoslovakia, Bishop Peter Janos of Hungary, Rev. Gustav Nystrom of Sweden, and Bishop Rajah Manikam of India. In their speeches, each of these men praised the Three-Self Movement and Bishop Manikam thought that the rest of the Christian world had much to learn from it!

One of the main themes of the conference concerned the action to be taken against the "counterrevolutionary elements in the churches." Mr. Y. T. Wu in his report compared the present work of the Three-Self Movement to that of the purification of the temple by Christ. He said that most of the churches had now joined the Three-Self Movement and that the reactionaries masquerading under the cloak of "faith" had been uncovered and arrested. There were still counterrevolutionary elements, however, in the churches, and they must be eliminated. He went on to report numerical increases in the churches, new publications put out by the official publishers, and the start of classes for political training. Ministers had also taken a share in social work and in the world peace movement. He declared that the main object before the Chinese church was unity. When the conference concluded, five days were taken up in Shanghai reporting what had taken place. All other main cities held similar follow-up conferences.

It was also in 1956 that Bishop K. H. Ting paid his visit to Europe, including London where, very plausibly, he expressed optimistic views for the future of the church in China. To those who knew the facts, however, his views seemed to be but a deceptive mirage.

Back in China, as if to bear out Bishop Ting's optimism, young people were still going to Bible schools. The churches were still carrying on, often in the absence of their regular ministers who were in prison. There was an unusual demand for Bibles which the Bible Society found it hard to meet. Evangelistic meetings in the Chinese New Year period were well attended and at one church there were 270 decisions. At special meetings in Chekiang eight hundred attended New Year meetings, some of the people coming from fifty English miles away, carrying their own bedding and other necessities. The authorities had been dubious about giving permission for the meetings, but finally provided a public hall and an army kitchen for catering purposes. Two Communist observers attended the meetings and were mystified by the atmosphere of joy. What made these people so happy? It was cold, and they had nothing special to eat! And yet they just sat there with their eyes closed, repeated, "Lord, Lord . . . Jesus, Jesus!" These meetings were the result of hundreds of conversions in the area through the witness of a Christian layman. These were young converts enjoying Christian fellowship and a Bible ministry for the first time! There was also good news from a tribal area in Kwangsi where, early in the summer of 1957, an appeal was received from a church in Nanning to go out to the Tung tribe. A three-day mountain journey brought the Chinese visitors to an area where a total of 433 persons from sixteen villages were baptized and a church organization set up. Some of these people had been waiting for twelve years for baptism. One of the first believers was a woman in her fifties, and among those baptized were several white-haired old men who said that they now felt like saying with Simeon: "Now lettest thou thy servant depart in peace, according to thy word: for mine eyes have seen thy salvation."

In the absence of regular pastors, many of whom were in prison, God seemed to be raising up most unlikely people to shepherd His sheep. There was a simple carpenter in the province of Chekiang, a humble vegetable-seller in another place, and a woman in the vicinity of Shanghai to whom Christians flocked when their fourteen churches were closed. The Christian Book Room was asked to supply hundreds of copies of *Words of Comfort* to these people.

Another encouraging event took place on October 8, 1956, when Dr. Chai Yu-ming's Spiritual Training College, which had been closed for some time, reopened as a new Union School with the China Christian Preachers Training Institute and the Grace Church Extension Seminary, all conservative Bible schools. All four members of the school administration were leading evangelicals, including Rev. Yang Shao-tang. The Peking branch of Dr. Chia's school, under the leadership of Miss Pi Yung-chin, had already become one of the component parts of the Union Yenching Theological Seminary.

In spite of all this, there was an atmosphere of anxiety as the ferreting out of counterrevolutionaries proceeded. A general feeling prevailed among Christians that all was not going well. On March 19, 1957, the Rev. Marcus Cheng made a startling speech before the Chinese People's Political Consultative Conference in Peking. This highly critical speech was surprisingly reported in full in the March 25 issue of *People's Daily* and, even more surprisingly, was reprinted in the May 13 issue of *Heavenly Wind*. The following extracts indicate the character of the speech:

> Some churches have not been allowed to resume services. In some villages and small cities church buildings and furniture have been appropriated by various government organs and the religious life of Christians interfered with. The policy [of the government] has not been uniform and some cadres have taken a hostile attitude throughout, forbidding subscribing money to the church, repairing church buildings, or taking in new members. Some cadres have not only not respected religious faith, but have even adopted an abusive attitude. . . . The contradiction between belief and unbelief, between atheism and theism, is a contradiction among the people and not against an external element. We are all citizens of China and this is not a contradiction between friends and enemies of the people. . . . It

is a contradiction of the "hundred schools." . . . You speak out your atheism and I will preach my theism, and in this controversy you must not take to abusing my mother, defiling my ancestral graves, or reviling my ancestors. In the eyes of us Christians, God is the Supreme Being and the churches are His temples, the place where Christians worship Him. In the argument over theism and atheism, you must not revile God or blaspheme His name; you must not take churches by force. For example, a letter from a minority tribesman just the other day says: "Our church is still occupied and is in a terrible condition and it is being used as a stable." This defiling of churches is like defiling our ancestral graves and impresses us very painfully. At the opening of a new steel bridge, an official of high rank gave an address in which he emphasized that this bridge had been made by human effort and was not the work of any so-called God. Then he said, "You Christians should throw your God into the dung heap." Such blasphemy of God is, in the eyes of Christians, worse than reviling one's mother. This is not criticism, but abuse of religion.

Words like these must have left the conference stunned to silence. They came from a Party member, a member of the Consultative Committee, a man who had gone far as any Christian could go and much farther than most had been prepared to go, the second in command to Y. T. Wu in the Three-Self Movement. No words could better express the disillusionment of many Christians with the direction things were taking. Marcus Cheng also criticized the anti-religious literature current in China. He must have known that such vitriolic criticism would bring about his own downfall. Was he perhaps making an attempt to atone for his past mistakes and for all he had done to bring about the downfall of so many of his fellow Christians, not the least of whom was Wang Ming-tao?

Chapter 10

BRAINWASHING

B RAINWASHING is a picturesque term by now well known. The Christian term "repent" suggests a change of mind, a putting away of wrong thoughts and attitudes to make room for new ones. The Communist technique called brainwashing is of a similar nature. All reactionary, imperialistic ideas must be washed clean out of the mind before the new truths of materialism and socialism can find their place there. But, unlike Christian repentance, this process is a frightening form of thought-control carried out under terrific psychological pressures. For a Christian to remain sane and faithful to his religious convictions after years of such pressures is a miracle in itself!

Ever since the Communists came to power they have been conducting the most thoroughgoing re-education of the whole population of China. The feat of organization involved is stupendous, for the task of re-educating a population of six hundred million people goes on daily. Every unit of society—workers in an office, children in a class at school, workers in a shop, at a factory, residents in a street, soldiers in a platoon—meet daily, in most cases out of work hours and, under the guidance of an instructed Communist, study dialectical materialism in all its facets and its ever-changing application to current events. One would need to be a very well-taught Christian to maintain an un-flinching stand after the first few weeks of the daily, inces-sant, inexorable bombardment of the mind with Marxist ideas. Yet Christians have been subjected to this continually for over ten years. Inevitably their thinking is, in many respects, being remolded—unconsciously so. For no one can escape these regular "study" sessions. Nor is it possible to hide one's true beliefs and convictions for very long from the leader of the group. The Christians soon become marked people. This kind of indoctrination has been the common lot of Christians and non-Christians alike. But for Christians it has been found necessary to institute special study classes, particularly for church leaders.

The Government has always interpreted the freedom of religious belief clause in the Constitution as giving them also the freedom to oppose religious beliefs. In the Peking *Daily Worker* there appeared an article in 1956 which openly attacked religion as superstitious and superfluous, and went on:

> Red China is engaged in achieving a perfect socialist state in a short time. Our welfare depends neither upon God nor upon His benefactions, nor does it depend on Buddha and his mercy. . . . Although there is no longer any religious belief among many, there are still some vestiges of the same among workers who should know that religion is really harmful to them. . . . What is more, counterrevolutionaries exploit these beliefs in the workers' world in order to foment their plots against the State. It is thus clear that we cannot adopt a laissez faire attitude toward religion. . . . The most important thing is to destroy the roots from which religion grows.

On January 3 Peking Radio stated that public school teachers must be responsible for making sure that their pupils are brought up as materialists and to see the evils of religious superstition.

In May 1957 there occurred a very significant and far-reaching event. The President of China and Chairman of the Party, Mao-Tze-tung, believing that everything in

China was now well under control, decided to lift the restrictions on free speech just a little. He thought that there was a place for constructive criticism of the regime, and, borrowing an old Chinese proverbial saying, decreed: "Let a hundred flowers bloom and let a hundred schools of thought contend!"—a picturesque way of saying, "Let every man express his own views!" Few can have anticipated the result. There was in fact a sudden outburst of pent-up feeling from all over China, particularly from the intellectual and student classes. Leading men in the Government made outspoken and very critical speeches about the way things had been going. No one was sacrosanct and even the highest in the land came in for criticism. Students all over China set up organizations, went on strike, circulated anti-Party propaganda, attacked Party officials, stuck up posters and demonstrated in the streets. At one middle school in Hanyang, students rioted for two days, attacking the arsenal, the electric power plant, the jail, and the Party headquarters. As a result three ringleaders were executed before ten thousand people, and others were sent to prison.

Naturally, Christians were not silent either and, like Marcus Cheng, some aired their grievances too freely.

The Government realized that it had made a grave mistake—unless the whole thing had been a deliberately calculated trap for the unwary! In July the Party struck back and a new campaign against reactionaries, now called "rightists," was launched. This was a purge conducted on the basis of the information which the short-lived freedom of speech had brought to light. The tables were turned on the critics, for it was evident that there was far more reactionary and anti-government and anti-socialist feeling among students and educated people than anyone had suspected. So began the prolonged "rectification campaign" designed to ferret out rightists and to correct their thinking. After seven years of it, the brainwashing had not proved sufficiently successful, even among the youth of the country who had been the most thoroughly indoctrinated. The process was therefore intensified.

Throughout the country Communist organizations began to fight against rightists in every level of society and to expose all who were still out of sympathy with Communism. In August a countrywide campaign against rightists within the church was launched. *Heavenly Wind* for August and September reported denunciations of rightists in various parts of the country, and as the list of names given lengthened with each succeeding number it became apparent that it included many of the foremost evangelicals in the church. A conference in Peking in December, under the direction, be it noted, of Communist Party leaders, produced a new spate of accusations. Christian ministers freely accused one another and sometimes themselves of all sorts of crimes against the regime. Eighty-year-old Dr. Chia Yu-ming was accused by two hundred of his fellow ministers and his license to preach was withdrawn. After this conference there were numerous arrests and many younger men were sent to jail. Any shred of leniency with those who had been reluctant to join in with the Three-Self Movement had long since disappeared. The one crime now was to be outside the Movement. The conference decided that the political education of all church workers left much to be desired and a long intensive series of study courses was decided upon. The leaders of the conference, who in this case were Communists and not even professing Christians, made it perfectly clear that the church was under the control of the Communist Party and that all Christian activities must be under the control of the official Three-Self Movement. No private gatherings could be tolerated. Thus the year 1957 ended in a mood of appre-

hension as to what 1958 might bring. The evangelical wing
of the church had suffered a heavy blow.

A trial course of study had already been held in Hankow
in 1954 and others had probably taken place from time to
time since then. But there had been nothing so intensive
and so searing to compare with the study courses in 1958.
The first Shanghai class was held in the well-known Union
Church near the Whangpoo River. Sessions took place
daily from Monday to Friday and lasted all day. The Government provided the midday meal. All church activities
except the Sunday services were canceled for the duration.
The first course lasted for three months, then another
group took the place of the first. During the endless lec-
tures and discussions on political and kindred subjects,
there was much bitter discussion. Mutual criticism was
deliberately stirred up. In consequence, several outstanding men were removed from their churches and so silenced.
Others were placed on probation. Some were sent to the
country to take part in the current "back to the land"
campaign in order to reform themselves by labor. While
the special courses were going on in Shanghai, others were
being conducted elsewhere. *Heavenly Wind* published in
full detail all the evils reportedly brought to light both in
the established denominations and among the sects. Even
after the intensive courses had ended pastors had continued
attending three or four classes a week. Arrests and dis-
missals became commonplace. Church leaders were be-
wildered.

In August, the Church of England Lambeth Conference
took place in London. Bishop K. H. Ting was expected
to be back with six or seven brother bishops to attend. But
at the opening of the conference a telegram from Bishop
Ting was read publicly. The contents read to the effect
that he and his colleagues were sorry not to be present
but they were too preoccupied with their tasks in China

to find time to attend. It would clearly have been embarrassing, especially for Bishop Ting, to revisit Great Britain. A year of increasing pressures and decreasing freedom, of intensive indoctrination and sweeping purges, would have made it impossible for the Bishop to maintain the fiction that the church in China was free and flourishing.

The anti-rightist campaign came to a head in October. So many young people were going to prison that Christians in the universities and colleges would take leave of one another with the words, "See you 'inside' next time!" One girl, when they came to arrest her, held out her hands for the handcuffs with the words, "I am not worthy!" Through the witness of Christians in prison some were being converted. One young man was offered release if only he would stop praying—an evidence of an unbalanced mind! But he preferred to stay in prison and pray.

At the end of November an enlarged session of the Executive Committee of the Three-Self Movement met in Peking. There were 130 representatives of Protestant churches present and the purpose of the meeting was, of course, to expose rightist thinking within the church. Five prominent leaders, all of whom had been official delegates to the second national conference of the Movement in 1954, were among those who were denounced. Most significant of all was the denunciation of the Rev. Marcus Cheng, a vice-chairman of the Movement, by his colleagues Mr. Y. T. Wu and eight other prominent leaders for the speech he had made at the People's Political Conference in March. This speech, said Mr. Wu, slandered the Communist Party and the People's Government of China and defamed the Three-Self Movement. His charge that Communist actions had been "worse than digging up our ancestors' graves" was the greatest defamation ever made against the Communist Party, against the Constitution, and the religious policy of the Government. Mr. Cheng's attitude was declared to be one of gross ingratitude, for it had been the Party and the People who had elected him as a member of the Political Affairs Committee and it was members of the Three-Self Movement who had provided him with his house and garden and all necessary supplies. While Mr. Cheng had been held in respect by church workers generally, he had repaid them with hatred for their favors!

This conference was intended to be a model for nationwide conferences on the provincial, district, and local levels. Every issue of *Heavenly Wind* reported the proceedings of long conferences on education in socialism, gave details of accusations against rightists, and described street parades and public oath-swearing ceremonies at which Christians reaffirmed the loyalty of the churches to Mao Tze-tung and the Communist Party. Remorselessly the campaigns dragged on. The True Jesus Church, an indigenous sect and one of the largest single denominations in China, came under heavy fire. Many leaders were denounced as counterrevolutionaries and dishonest rascals. The Rev. Yang Shao-tang, who had once been a prominent Three-Self leader, had recently paid a visit to his native province of Shansi. He had naturally revisited the churches where he had once worked as their pastor. Imagine his dismay, therefore, when, on his return to Shanghai, he was accused, illogically, of trying to revive the ill-famed China Inland Mission! What distressed him most was that his own students at the Spiritual Life Seminary were the foremost in accusing him. He was sent away for a period of "reform by labor." When he returned home, he was but a shadow of his former self and somewhat affected in mind too. The story of Yang Shao-tang is an illustration of the way in which the Three-Self leaders have used people for their own ends and then, when there was no further use for them, have discarded them. Three outstanding Methodist and Lutheran pastors in Hunan were denounced. Episcopal Bishop Stephen Chang and fourteen other Christian leaders were denounced. Six well-known leaders in Anhwei were denounced during a seventy-day study course at which "a stern struggle was waged against these elements through the production of facts." Dr. Chia Yu-ming and forty of his graduates were among seven hundred Christians who were imprisoned about Christmastime. One of Dr. Chia's former lecturers was a young woman who had refused to respond to indoctrination. She and her companion were therefore sent up to the northwest, to the Chinese "Siberia." In the bitter cold of winter and with inadequate clothing they had to live in a flimsy hut and were employed in gathering firewood on the bleak hills. When one of them began to suffer from exposure and poor food, she was allowed to remain "at home" and to make cloth shoes. Later she was reported to have been moved to the mines in Central Asia. Hundreds of Christians have been similarly banished. When Dr. Luther Shao, head of the Disciples of Christ Church, was denounced in 1958, he is said to have committed suicide. There is no end to such tragic reports.

What of Christians who were condemned to long terms of imprisonment? How did they bear up under the trial? Among several interesting reports, one from an independent witness is of special interest. Mr. A. P. Friedlander, a White Russian businessman in Tientsin and a Christian, was released in August 1957 after six years' imprisonment. As a result of the tortures he had suffered, he had a crack in his hip and a broken wrist which had been allowed to heal without medical help. He said that he had met many Chinese Christians in prison, both Protestant and Roman Catholic, and he was full of praise for their loyalty and sense of unity. They were there for "ideological remolding," and their captors tried their best to break their spirits by persecution. They were denied the right to pray or even to have a Bible, yet they managed to carry on secretly. He himself was often able to strengthen the faith of weaker brethren by talking to them of the Saviour's sufferings and of His ultimate glory.

The Apostle Paul, who had himself endured much at the hands of his opponents, continually emphasizes in his epistles the necessity for patient endurance in prolonged trials. If it were not for this assurance that God never allows any trial to exceed a Christian's power of endurance, we might easily be led to think that the sufferings of Chinese Christians are more than flesh and blood can endure. But in the great eleventh chapter on faith in the Epistle to the Hebrews, it is said of Moses that, under the prolonged testing of his faith in the wilderness, he endured as seeing Him who is invisible. It is only the vision of a crucified, risen, and ascended Saviour that will enable Chinese believers to endure to the end!

Chapter 11

STRANGLEHOLD

MR. CHOU EN-LAI, Premier of China, in his initial discussions in 1950 with church leaders, had specifically said that denominational distinctions must go and the church must unite. There is no doubt that this official directive has been the goal of the Three-Self leaders from the very beginning, although they were forced to soft-pedal this aspect of things in the early stages of their program.

The original name of the Movement included the word "reform" and when Christians were suspicious of this, it had to be omitted. Mr. Y. T. Wu repeatedly reassured the leaders of the different churches that there was no intention of interfering with the internal affairs of the churches. In August 1954 Mr. Wu, in his report to the second conference of the Three-Self Movement, went out of his way to say:

> The purpose of the Three-Self Movement is to unite the Christian church in China. Self-government does not mean to unify or modify the organization of the various churches. . . . Self-support is not to interfere in the finances of any church. . . . The purpose of self-propagation is not to unify or modify the creeds. . . . We should respect the differences that exist among the churches in creed, organization, and ritual.

But in so saying, Mr. Wu was being less than honest. Two years later, in March 1956, at a conference in Peking, Mr. Wu stated that the first object before the church was unity—all barriers which separated Christians from one another and the church from the world must be removed. Bishop K. H. Ting, in his address at the Y.M.C.A., in London on July 3, 1956, said: "Recently the denominations have been in very close association. There is no organized church union. The special character of each denomination has not been trespassed upon, but there is unity in the way of Christian obedience." Not many months later, however, it was reported that the Three-Self Movement was insisting, under pressure from the Government, on the union of all Protestant bodies, whatever their ecclesiastical differences might be.

The "Hundred Flowers" episode shook the nation and gave birth to the rectification campaign. This served to increase suspicion of any who had not by then thrown in their lot with the Three-Self Movement. Toward the end of the year apprehension grew and there was a feeling that big changes were to take place in 1958. The year began with the special courses for Christian workers, already described. The Christian press reported with monotonous regularity denunciations and convictions of rightists in the church. Many Christians were in prison. Wang Ming-tao retracted his confession, and he and Mrs. Wang returned to their prison cells.

In the autumn, the "commune" system was introduced throughout the entire rural areas of China. In September rapid developments took place within the churches. They were now ordered to effect a real union. To simplify this process, large numbers of churches were closed. Many cities were left with no choice of a place of worship. Some were allowed two churches. Peking, the capital, which had had about eighty churches, was left with four, one for each point of the compass. It was argued that the churches were not full and there was no need for so many different buildings. Actually there were about twenty thousand Christians in Peking, but owing to Sunday being the day when youth organizations held their meetings, when parades were organized, and when housewives attended to the tasks for which they had no time on other days, not more than a quarter of the Christians were able to attend church. In the cities, Sunday had been turned into the jolliest day of a lack-luster week, though in the communes there were only two rest days a month. In Shanghai, where there had once been over two hundred churches serving a city of three million people, the number was reduced to about twenty.

On the first Sunday after the enforced union, sermons were preached throughout the churches which called for rejoicing in the light and blessing that had now come to Christians.

As far as the church was concerned, the anti-rightist drive took a new turn in 1958. The emphasis was shifted to the "illegal activities" within the church—such activities as free-lance preaching or holding private meetings in homes, a practice to which Christians had been driven by circumstances. *Heavenly Wind* for March 31 listed the five resolutions made by one group of churches in Shanghai: "We will not break the laws. We will not preach reactionary doctrine. We will not try to get people to become Christians on the plea that Christ can heal the sick. We will not invite free-lance evangelists to preach in our churches. We will not attend or preach in underground services in homes." These are typical of the resolutions passed by many similar meetings elsewhere. One church in Manchuria promised to divide its members into three classes: the patriotic, those needing education, and the "bad elements"! They would expel the last group and educate the second. Further, they promised to investigate the patriotic attitude of every applicant for baptism!

Meanwhile it was being taught that denominations had been a deliberately planned method of keeping missionaries in control of the churches and so perpetuating imperialist influences. Any nominal autonomy of church organizations had been just a facade. This was said to be true both of denominational churches and of the interdenominational bodies like the China Inland Mission, where control used to be directly in the hands of the missionaries. The declared purpose of the Three-Self Movement was now to free the churches from this "imperialist and semi-colonial" status. However, they still denied any intention of changing the doctrines of the church or of altering the constitution, organization, or traditions of any branch of the church.

The union of all the churches was not at first effected on a nationwide basis. Local union was first sought. From August onward, the religious press contained accounts of the process in city after city. The work was in the hands of the local committee of the Three-Self Movement. The representatives of each denomination took upon themselves the responsibility of formally surrendering to the Three-Self Committee all their property and the control of their church program. Then they voted themselves out of existence. Some of these unions produced strange associations. In two provinces, the union of churches seems to have been carried out by the provincial headquarters of the several churches working in the area.

An example of how union took place is provided by the case of Taiyuan, the provincial capital of Shansi. The articles of union read:

> There shall be unified worship for the city of Taiyuan and a ministerial staff of three or four. All fellow workers besides these and those assigned to the Three-Self office shall throw themselves into the socialist construction of our mother country; those who are old or physically weak shall retire. All real and movable

church property and all church funds shall be turned over to the Three-Self Patriotic Committee.

Church Organization:

1. All former governing committees and boards of the various churches are hereby abolished and the administration of the church shall be in the hands of the Three-Self Patriotic Committee.

2. Regarding ritual, regulations and church order:

(a) There shall be a unified worship program and each church shall surrender its own individual ritual.

(b) The hymns used in worship shall be unified and a committee shall choose and edit hymns for use.[1]

(c) All books used in the interpretation of the Bible shall be examined and judged and those containing poisonous thoughts shall be rejected. Only teachings favoring union and socialism shall be used. In particular any material coming from outside China shall be carefully examined before being accepted.

(d) There shall be no more preaching about the Last Day or about the vanity of this world. This is negative and pessimistic teaching. Instead we shall emphasize the need for the union of faith and practice, the dignity of labor, the control of nature and the dividing line between ourselves and our enemies, between right and wrong.

(e) Belief and unbelief shall not be made an issue in determining marriage questions.

3. In regard to the necessary reform of each church:

(a) The Little Flock shall abolish its women's meet-

---

[1] Sample of a new political hymn added to the hymnbook:
Thanks to the Communist Party and President Mao,
For after Liberation the Church has been united;
We are no longer divided into denominations;
We are no longer divided into those who have and have not;
We have self-propagation, self-support, and self-government;
We are not now oppressed by imperialism;
Our standard of living has been raised;
We live in a society which is free and happy.

ings, its weekly breaking of bread, its personal interviews with members before the breaking of bread, and its rule against women speaking in church.

(b) The Salvation Army shall give up all its military regulations.

(c) The Seventh Day Adventists shall abolish their daily morning prayers. On the sabbath they shall participate in beneficial good works and economic production. Their tithe system for the support of the clergy shall be abolished and also their unification of accounts for Shansi Province.

(d) All the Y.M.C.A. secretaries shall be assigned to productive labor and the closing of the Taiyuan Y.M.C.A. as a separate organization shall be carefully considered.

It is evident that a large amount of property and much of the church personnel were thus released from the service of the church and became available to the State in its all-absorbing drive for industrial power. The large Little Flock church in Shanghai and the Anglican cathedral in Peking are known to have become factories. Gone to the wind were the denials of any intent to unify or interfere with the internal affairs or to modify the liturgy and practices of the different churches!

And the process of denunciation went relentlessly on and on! In November, seven Swatow leaders were denounced and arrested. In Shanghai, three of the Little Flock pastors who had been imprisoned since 1956 were sentenced to severe prison terms—two to fifteen years and one to twelve years. Yang Shao-tang, once high in the Three-Self hierarchy, and a man who had repeatedly suffered at the hands of the leaders of the Movement, came in for fresh criticism in October. He was accused of being two-faced and, though publicly condemning reactionaries like Wang Ming-tao, he had secretly supported them. In

November a group of Three-Self leaders in Shanghai issued a statement referring to church workers denounced during the previous year:

> These landlords, rich farmers, reactionaries, bad elements and rightists who have been hidden within the church have used the cloak of religion and, with faith as a pretext, have stressed the difference between theism and atheism in order to carry on anti-Party and anti-socialist activities. They use every legal and illegal opportunity to preach against the Government's important campaigns. Among the former exploiting classes and disillusioned elements they use prayer and family gatherings to tempt them to resist change. Some good church members have been deluded by them and led to take part in their reactionary activity.

On January 5, 1959, Mr. Y. T. Wu summed up the achievements of 1958, the year of great changes, in these words:

> We Christians during the past year have been deeply disciplined. Through socialist education the clergy and the laity of the whole country have had their thinking raised to a new level: the rightists have been decisively defeated; the semi-colonial aspect of the church has been changed; and the Chinese church is now in process of shaking off the shackles of imperialism and ready to advance on the road to socialism.

The interpretation of this statement is that the Government had successfully placed a stranglehold on the church. The original Government aim had been achieved. The prophetic words of Wang Ming-tao had come to pass: *"If the church should ever be reduced to such a state, though there were Sunday services and other formalities, she would in fact have already been liquidated."*

Chapter 12

WHAT OF THE NIGHT?

In August 1958, the Chinese Government embarked on the most colossal social experiment ever undertaken. Immediate interest was created all around the world. Much hung on the success or failure of the scheme.

Many years ago, Karl Marx, the prophet of Communism, foresaw entire populations being organized into industrial and agricultural armies; as a result production would be raised to unheard-of levels. Socialism, whose slogan is, "From each according to his ability, to each according to his work," would then move forward to Communism with the slogan, "From each according to his ability, to each according to his need." One hundred per cent nationalization or collectivization, even of the home life and personal possessions of the individual, would, it was believed, result in such abundance of every kind that Karl Marx's Utopia would be speedily ushered in.

In the early years of the Russian Revolution, the Soviet Republic had made a brief but disastrous trial of the commune system. The resulting famine cost over a million lives. Undaunted by this example and with a growing independence of Russian advice, China went ahead with her plans. The aim of the communes is maximum production in every sphere. To this end, every individual in the nation, except the very young and the very old, is conscripted into a commune. All the activity of the commune is directed after the fashion of a military operation. Indeed, production is looked upon as a battle, a fight with nature. Home life is officially regarded as selfish, and an inefficient and uneconomical use of female labor; women are therefore set free from domestic chores in favor of productive labor by providing communal meals, communal laundries, communal tailors and, in some cases, communal sleeping places. The children from early infancy become the care of the State which provides crèches and later boarding arrangements in the schools for all. In reply to widespread criticism of the abolition of the traditional home life of the Chinese, articles appeared in Chinese magazines in December 1958 justifying the new arrangements and claiming that the people were thus being set free from their prison homes and that the children were now learning to regard the commune as both home and parent and receiving from the commune as much or more affection than from their own parents.

The pilot or "sputnik" commune was tried out in the province of Honan. Then, in the autumn of 1958, the experiment was extended to other parts of China. By September nine provinces had been communized and by December 10 it was claimed that ninety-nine per cent of all peasant households had been converted into communes. That is, five hundred million people found their ancient and traditional mode of life completely swept away! In the southwestern tribal areas the tribal minorities were forced into the same communes as the Chinese with a view to their complete integration. This led to violence and large numbers of tribespeople have been escaping across the border into Burma. Only the city populations for the time being remained outside this social revolution and continued a more or less normal existence.

The Chinese farmer who, a few years ago, had been gratified by a "land reform" which took land from the landlords and gave every peasant his own piece of land to till, later found *his* piece of land becoming part of a State "cooperative." That was bad enough, but now he found himself, his wife and children, his father and mother becoming mere units in a vast "collective," numbering from about 8,000 people to as many as 260,000, which is the size of one Manchurian commune. All must be ready to obey orders to engage in any kind of work—sometimes agricultural, sometimes industrial, perhaps building roads or repairing dikes, or it may be in a laundry brigade or in a tailoring brigade. Hours of work are often very long. Political studies fill "leisure" hours, while for the young there is also daily military drill. With only two rest days a month, there is little leisure time. The reward for this intensive labor is free provision of essential needs and the care of health, rather than cash wages. The existence of thirty or forty million militiamen has freed some of the armed forces for industrial work.

China has thus become a nation of desperately "busy ants." For, to catch up with the West, then to exceed it in production and to rival the West in exports to other countries, a stupendous effort is needed. So everyone must work, *work,* work and produce, *produce,* PRODUCE! Production targets were set very high and rewards were offered to communes attaining their targets. Statistics for 1958 showed a fantastic increase in both industrial and agricultural output. Steel production went up steeply as the result of a campaign to set up home-made smelters in every back yard.

Into this drive for production and the socialist transformation of the country the church was drawn. It was regarded as specially patriotic if a church voluntarily declared a complete recess of church activities during the busy farming seasons. Every minister and church worker was to be recruited to support the Great Leap Forward. Everyone was expected to volunteer to promise a certain number of days a year, averaging about fifty. For instance, in one province church workers contributed a total of 196 days of manual labor during September 1958 in the fields and factories or in building communications. This followed a provincial political study institute for religious workers. The same pattern took shape in other provinces. In Peking, most of the preachers spent six months in manual labor and then in January 1959 met to share their experiences and to discover in what ways they had been "changed through labor." The Government believes that hard manual labor is the most effective way to reform the bourgeois-and-capitalist-mentality and to wipe out the differences between workers and intellectuals.

From the very first there was strong opposition to the whole stupendous scheme. Many were the expressions of distrust and distaste. The tempo of the work resulted in general exhaustion, and the disruption of normal life brought about mental bewilderment. As time went on, it became increasingly apparent that the experiment was not going as well as expected. In the summer of 1959 China's top leaders met in conference in the lovely mountain resort of Kuling. The official report of their findings shocked the country, for it was the most serious confession of failure in the Communist world since the denigration of Stalin. Production figures had been grossly exaggerated and the "steel" produced in the much publicized back-yard furnaces was hardly steel at all and almost useless in industry. The quality of industrial products had been very poor. Labor had been unwisely used. Agriculture had suffered. The worst floods in a hundred years in the south, drought and pests in the north, aggravated the situation. Food shortages became acute. Rationing was strict in the large cities. Famine stalked abroad in some parts of the country. The confession that the Great Leap Forward to full scale Communism had got off to a bad start is proving a serious loss of face for China in the eyes of her Asian neighbors.

Modifications in the commune system have already been introduced and there are reports that some communes have actually been disbanded.

It needs little imagination to understand how the commune system will have affected rural churches. Inevitably the familiar pattern of church life has been broken up. With no regular Sundays, normal worship, when all Christians could meet together, has become impossible. Weeknight gatherings have ceased. Sunday schools are out of the question. With the break-up of family life, family worship is impossible. With the children in crèches or boarding schools, Christian parents can no longer bring up their own children "in the fear and admonition of the Lord." During 1958, some 45,000 school children were drafted away from their homes in Canton to the labor front to engage in production. From north China 15,000 children "gloriously left their home towns for the frontier provinces of the northwest." What of the Christian children among them?

Letters from a coastal city to relatives in Hong Kong illustrate the foregoing:

> Pastor X was condemned by the Communists as a rightist. He has been under the Communists' control and is not permitted to preach in our church. The attendance at Sunday worship grows less and less because all the people must serve the slavery work from dawn to dusk, about fifteen or sixteen hours every day. So far there are only a few very old women or men able to go to church to worship. My grandson has to help the farmers with the harvesting from 3 A.M. to 6 P.M., and after that he has to attend Communist doctrine meeting for one and a half to two hours. As he has been exhausted so bitterly he has now fallen into disease. The Communists have recently organized the so-called "Public Eating Society" here, and all church buildings are used as mass eating places to accommodate hun-

dreds of people eating together. Now the majority of
the families are destroyed by compelling the children
to live separately from their parents. When the people
gather for meals the Communists only supply two bowls
of rice. The vegetables must be provided by the eater
himself. A laborer receives $2 a month and pays $1 for
his rice.

A later letter from the same city added this news:

My children are forced to work in the cornfields for
eighteen hours daily and supplied with very rough food
without any nutrition. All people from a little child
under ten up to the age of eighty must take up daily
labor in the farming areas, and there are only two days
allowed for rest in their homes. All churches in this
city are closed!

The commune system has not yet been fully applied to
towns and cities, but this is yet to come and has already
affected some cities. The Great Leap Forward is proving
a tremendous strain on the economy of China and on her
longsuffering people. Naturally the Government holds
out the promise of undreamed plenty and prosperity and
increased amenities for all "in three years' time." Meanwhile everything is being sacrificed in the interests of the
State. The Christian church, as we have shown, is being
steadily crushed beneath the wheels of this juggernaut.
Christians, whatever they may feel, are not permitted to
speak of the darkness of the times, for is not China under
Communism "moving toward the dawn of a glorious new
day"?

The question that everyone is asking is, what future has
the Christian church in the New China? The reader will
have gathered that the church in its broadest sense is
deeply divided. The leaders of the official organization
appear in the role of inquisitors—they fully support the
Government, they have been successfully indoctrinated,

they soft-pedal the subject of atheism, they extol the Communist system and *kowtow* to their Communist rulers. They have gladly surrendered their hearts to the Communist Party and have lent themselves to be accusers of their brethren. Like Saul of Tarsus, they have made havoc of the church, binding and delivering into prisons both men and women and bringing them to be punished. They are backed by all the power of the State and have used every means at their disposal, from craft and intimidation to imprisonment and execution, to enforce conformity to their demands; these demands are nothing other than the dictates of the Government. Believers may no longer meet in private. Ministers faithful to God's Word and their own consciences are either dead, in prison, or deprived of their licenses to preach. A report from Shanghai at the end of 1958 said that "many are earning the crown of life."

Miss Willis, who succeeded in remaining in China longer than any other Protestant missionary, reached Hong Kong in May, 1959. She reported:

> Everyone lives in fear, except those who can entirely commit themselves to God, trusting that His way is perfect and that it is a privilege to suffer for Him. There are many such, but we need to pray that their faith may not grow weak under the lengthened trial. And the weaker a Christian is, the more he needs our prayers. Fear can so easily lead to compromise and compromise can lead anywhere, as it has already with some good men.
>
> There are those whose faith fails amid the long series of indoctrination meetings and they begin to doubt whether there is a God. One such, a mailman, was brought safely through and I heard him giving thanks that though he had often failed God, God had never failed him. There are also the many young and feeble Christians who, now that the churches are closed or preach only politics, have no food for their souls and

are spiritually starving to death. Some feel that by making a little compromise they can do so much more for God, though there is no doubt that they sincerely wish to serve Him. Others are almost in despair because every means of witness seems cut off from them and they are weighed down with the thought of the millions in the darkness around. These do what is most effectual—they meet frequently in twos and threes to pray, often with tears and with much earnestness. Then, though their lips may not speak and though they are forbidden to give away any literature, their lives shine with a light that cannot be hid—like the lady who had worked in a Christian hospital: when the Communists in 1958 finally ordered the hospital to close, the women of the district refused to let her go and she continued to live among them.

The betrayal of the church is now historic fact. But although there have been many Peters who, under pressure, have repeatedly denied Christ and contradicted their Christian loyalty, there have probably been but few Judases who, for sordid and selfish ends, have deliberately betrayed Christ and the brethren, bringing untold soul anguish and mental and physical suffering to the members of Christ's Body. Through the experiences of the church over the last ten years, the Devil has been sifting the church like wheat. There has been much chaff, but the pure wheat is there. What comfort they must derive from the words of Christ: "I have prayed for thee, that thy faith fail not"! Shall not we too pray this prayer?

It may well be asked, to what end is all this suffering? Does the Lord of the church ever permit the members of His body to suffer in vain and to no purpose? The cross provides the answer. To friends and foes alike, that lonely cross was "the end of it all"! It was utter defeat in the eyes of men—the victory of darkness and Hell! But that dark day and the three dark days in the tomb which followed were but the prelude to the glorious Resurrection morning! Defeat was then turned into victory! Hell, which had hitherto been on the offensive and at the cross had inflicted a "crippling blow" on its arch-Enemy, was hurled back into a defensive position before the enveloping armies of God. We have the authority of Christ that, though Hell should take cover within mighty walls and heavily armored gates, those gates will neither hold out indefinitely nor hold their captives forever! Faith sees beyond the present darkness to a new dawn for the church in China. We hear the cry, "Watchman, what of the night?" Back comes the answer: "The morning cometh, and also the night"!

The present dusk is not the dusk of day's end, but the dusk that precedes the dawn.

Date Due

DEC 3 74			
JUN 22 '78			
6/10/80			
JUN 24 '80			
APR 19 1990			
FEB 2 0 1995			
MAY 2 3 2006			